IN THE NET

An Internet Guide for Activists

Jim Walch

ZED BOOKS
London & New York

In the Net was first published by
Zed Books Ltd, 7 Cynthia Street, London N1 9JF, UK,
and Room 400, 175 Fifth Avenue, New York, NY 10010, USA in 1999

Distributed in the USA exclusively by St Martin's Press, Inc.,
175 Fifth Avenue, New York, NY 10010, USA

Copyright © Jim Walch 1999
jwalch@igc.apc.org
Logo on title page © Greennet

The right of Jim Walch to be identified as the author of this
work has been asserted by him in accordance with the Copyright,
Designs and Patents Act, 1988

Typeset in Monotype Garamond by Lucy Morton & Robin Gable, Grosmont
Cover designed by Andrew Corbett
Printed and bound in the United Kingdom
by Biddles Ltd, Guildford and King's Lynn

A catalogue record for this book is available from the British Library

Library of Congress Cataloging-in-Publication Data available

ISBN 1 85649 758 5 (Hb)
ISBN 1 85649 759 3 (Pb)

IN THE NET

About the Author

Jim Walch is dean of social science education at South Stockholm University College, Sweden, and the author of many books and journal articles on communications, education and Indian politics. A long-term cyberactivist, he is currently researching the confluence of information and communication technologies and global education.

Contents

Foreword

There was war in Europe in 1999. And – as is common in situations of armed conflict – there is more confusion than clarity. There was much media attention, but little reliable information. There was propaganda from both Serbia and NATO. Most foreign journalists had to leave Yugoslavia, with only a few remaining in Belgrade, and the independent radio station B92 in Belgrade was closed down. As during the Gulf War and the crises in Bosnia, China and Indonesia, one of the few sources of information was the Internet. The mainstream agencies such as CNN and BBC, alternative sources and the Serbian government disseminated news and opinions through their websites.

The trouble obviously is that both information providers and political propagandists have discovered the power of the Net. Often it is practically impossible to distinguish genuine information from lies or just rumours. In this context, Jim Walch's chapter on Networking in a War Zone is indeed very timely and relevant. The use of the Net in war situations demonstrates that computer-communications technology, like any technology, is a mixed blessing. Technology always serves different and often conflicting purposes. Since the Greeks delivered us the myth of Prometheus – who stole the fire from the Gods on Olympus and thus brought progress – we should know that technology brings both benefits to humankind and the anger of Zeus.

This book is about the progressive uses of electronic networking: the use of computer-mediated communication in the struggle for global humanization. In his analysis of the technological potential, Walch has provided a very useful account of the opportunities the new technology offers for social activism in the service of human empowerment. He has supported his argument with well-documented and pertinent case-studies. It is important that he has not done this in a naive manner. He is aware of the risks and drawbacks and is not ready to be enthralled by fashionable net-hypes. This is essential since facile partisanship with either the 'cyberphiles' or the 'cyber-phobes', the techno-optimists or the techno-pessimists, is not at all helpful.

It is fascinating to see how a technology with strong military roots, primarily designed and developed to support centralized, bureaucratic structures and to serve largely destructive purposes, evolved into an instrument used for interactive communications within almost anarchistic environments and for constructive, progressive purposes. The same technology, however, is also deployed worldwide in efforts that contribute to dehumanization, not only in acts of cyberterrorism or hate propaganda in the support of ethnic cleansing, but also through such extensive surveillance programmes as are operated by the US National Security Agency.

I believe – as does Jim Walch – that Net technology has extraordinary potential for human empowerment. I also believe, however, that the realization of this potential will depend not upon features of the technology itself, but upon the political decisions and the institutional arrangements that govern their deployment. The present dominant governance structures – through fora like the World Trade Organization and its policies on the trade of telecom services and the protection of intellectual property rights – do not augur well for an equitable accessibility of the technology and a deployment thereof inspired by public interest motives.

There is today a worldwide trend for governments to delegate the responsibility for basic social choices to the marketplace. The democratic control of important social domains is thus increasingly eroded without any major societal debate. Following their desire to deregulate, liberalize and privatize, many governments are leaving the governance of the new Information and Communications Technologies (ICTs) in the hands of private entrepreneurs. One implication is that the realization of the development potential of ICTs comes to depend more upon investment decisions than upon considerations of common welfare.

Walch is aware of the political context as he writes 'The world of cyber-whatever is severely framed by real politics in a very real world.'

In connection with this he very aptly refers to electricity. This is indeed the key resource for the future development of ICTs. The fact that more and more countries are handing over the provision of electricity to forces of the so-called free market holds bleak prospects for both affordable access and optimal quality of services. From countries that have recently privatized their energy provision come worrying reports of increases in consumer prices and a decrease in levels of service and technical security.

The necessary sequel to the present book would have to take a critical look at the current global governance of new information and communication technologies and at the ways in which social activists can begin to change this. Walch observes that 'alternative technology presupposes a movement toward an alternative society'. Since the very same technology will also be deployed for non-emancipatory purposes, the essential question is whether progressive citizens can mobilize a global civil movement that is sufficiently strong not only to resist regressive movements but even to take the lead in actions towards a more humane world in the twenty-first century.

The greatest obstacle in this process is the lethargic majority of uninterested citizens. As Lord Acton once observed, the reason why evil can triumph is the 'good men who do nothing'. The greatest challenge at the turn of the century is to use the new interactive communication capabilities to wake the 'good men and women' out of their complacent slumber and make them realize that without their active intervention the third millennium offers little to look forward to.

Cees J. Hamelink, Amsterdam

Preface

It is hard to say when I started work on this book. Perhaps it was when I got my first computer and modem in 1983 and started communicating electronically at excruciatingly slow speeds. Or maybe it was two years later when I started experimenting with a simple BBS (Bulletin Board System) that eventually developed into PeaceNet Sweden and later NordNet. Or when such networks serving alternative movements around the world joined together in 1990 to form the APC, the Association for Progressive Communications. Thanks to the generous support from the Swedish Council for Planning and Coordination of Research (Forskningsrådsnämnden, FRN), I have been able to devote time to research and systematic reflection over experiences gained in the field.

Since I have been actively involved in the construction of an informational and communications infrastructure for social movements, I have a keen interest in finding out if such computer-mediated communication makes a difference. And if so, what kind of difference. So in one sense, this book is an evaluation of some of the work I and many others have been involved in. These 'others' are the *communications activists*. In this book I will argue that computer-mediated communication is a new field of social activity, sustained by a community of activists. This is a community, with a special ethic and way of doing things. A most fascinating aspect of working with the progressive application of computer-mediated communication has been witnessing the creative synergy released when socially and politically aware computer technicians start working with technically aware movement people.

This is not a technological or organizational study but action research on examples of how information and communication technology is actually being used for progressive social change. Organizational studies and materials are usually available in and around the organizations themselves – nowadays in colourful on-line World Wide Web presentations. There is a growing body of literature dealing with the effects of information and communication technology. Much is at the micro-level, even though some macro-studies are beginning to appear. This study takes a more contextual approach: the new technology is seen as part of a political process. The perspective is that of 'alternative' experimentation. The content is based on examples. These examples are dramatic. The idea behind this type of presentation is that extreme situations may often bring out dimensions that, while present, may be hidden in everyday situations.

There are several very good 'hands-on' guides to alternative electronic communications: Graham Lane's *Communications for Progress* (1990), Burkhard Luber's *The World at Your Keyboard* (1993) and *@t ease with email,* from the UN NGLS and the Friedrich Ebert Stiftung (1995). *Van Bolwerken tot Netwerken* (1994, Dutch for *From Bulwarks to Networks*) by Michael Polman and Peter van der Pouw Kraan adds on to the 'how to' approach with analysis, argumentation and exemplification of the uses of computer-mediated communication by social movements. A similar approach is used by Lars Truedson in his *Internet för en bättre värld* (1997, Swedish for *Internet for a Better World*). *Working Together Online* by Maureen James and Liz Rykert (1997) explains how to do just that, moving from the two-hands-on approach to many hands joining electronically.

A new technology brings with it new terminology. While I have attempted to keep the text as free as possible from computerese, some terms that may be unfamiliar are unavoidable. To worsen things, some terms are under controversy and undecided. For example, what should the new technology be called? The new technology being computers plus modems, cables and telephones and other equipment. Instead of using the term Information Technology (IT), which may include all forms of media that convey information, the term has been specified into Information and Communications Technology (ICT). The term I feel most comfortable with is Computer-Mediated Communication (CMC), though those working within a broadcasting frame of mind might feel left out of this definition. Since this book is not a polemic about these definitions, they will be intermixed. I have used a layout technique of creating a number 'info-boxes' in the text. These are used to refine some concepts as well as provide space for illustrative examples. There are a number of websites presented in order to illustrate and strengthen examples of how ICT is being used. (These sites, like the other Internet sources in the book, are dated 1997–98 unless otherwise stated.)

A basic starting point is that networks are people. Electronic networks are not 'there' until they are used. As will be apparent from the text, the experiences related and analysed here are shared experiences. And I can hardly start to name all those who have provided information, insights and criticisms in my work of gathering and sifting. However, some special thanks to netweavers Michael Polman of Antenna in Nijmegen, for listening and providing many fruitful insights; to Mika Böök in Helsinki, for breaking ground; to Eric Bachman, ZaMir Transnational Net, for sticking with it, and for fruitful comments and sharing of insights, most of which are incorporated in the text; to Burkhard Luber of the Threshold Foundation in Ottersberg, Germany; to APC co-founder Ian Peter down in Australia; and to Fritz Florin in Culemburg, the Netherlands.

The book is organized in five chapters. Chapter 1, 'Getting Started', intends to do just that by presenting an orientation to the struggle over the mode of information and ways of relating to the new information and communications technology. This chapter also presents my framework of analysis and how I approach this type of politics of information technology. Chapter 2, 'Going for IT', is mainly a history of how computers, computing and electronic networking have been liberated from governments and corporations. A brief typology of emancipatory networks is presented, as well as some more widely known effects of computer-mediated communication. Chapter 3, 'Networking in a War Zone', is a case study of how computer-mediated communication has been used in Bosnia and other parts of former Yugoslavia by peace and humanitarian organizations. The time frame is 1991–95. Chapter 4, 'Examples of Better Uses of Electronic Networking', picks up some threads from the case of former Yugoslavia and weaves out to a dozen examples of different types of progressive uses of electronic networking. Chapter 5, 'Computer Support for Emancipatory Action', examines differentiation within the community of communications activists. The conclusion to the book is a discussion of what the expansion of the new technology, expanding access to it and restrictions on this technology might mean.

1

Getting Started

Under what conditions do technologies tend to be shaped and used better rather than worse?

Edward Woodhouse

The 1997 Nobel Peace Prize was awarded to the International Campaign to Ban Landmines. On the day the award was announced, a Swedish organizer and board member of the ICBL, Carl von Essen, representing Save the Children, was interviewed on Swedish Radio. When asked why he thought the campaign had been awarded the Prize, he replied spontaneously that it was because the campaign was an effective, non-hierarchical organization thanks to electronic communications.[1]

One widely discussed and hoped for 'better' use of information technology would be to strengthen democracy. This is sometimes expressed as a means for bolstering existing structures and patterns in the polity, sometimes as an expanding citizenship in cyberspace – by which is meant access to the technologies of information, not just as a passive consumer but as a traveller in cyberspace, freely searching, producing and communicating. This hope for a 'better' democratizing use of information technology needs to be tempered by the insight that democracy, be in it cyber- or any other space, does not just happen or grow out of the ground like grass along a garden path. Democracy has to be won, often after a long struggle, and protected when gained. A starting point here is the assumption that 'democracy in one country' is no longer a viable tenet. We need a global perspective. Struggles are borne up by real people in the real world – not in any virtual world. Democracy has a content. This content is not only the right to vote but also human freedoms and rights. Among these are the right to life and freedom from exploitation, both of which are constantly threatened by war, environmental degradation and oppressive economic and political regimes.

This study focuses on how computer-mediated communication is being used in the global struggle for humanization.[2] The actors here are the communications activists, working in and around non-governmental organizations, movements and groups. While working on the fringes of political power structures, they are addressing the issues of planetary survival concerning the environment, peace, human rights, sustainable development and an equitable distribution of global resources. They are experimenting in 'better' or 'alternative' uses of modern information technology – an experimentation rooted in social *praxis*. 'Alternative' does not mean 'outside' or cut off from the mainstream. On the contrary, the meaning of alternative, as integrated utopia, is contained as part and parcel of the mainstream, its unutilized or underutilized component.[3] This can be stated in another way.

An obvious, common-sense place to look for 'better' uses of the new information and communications technology is in social movements that use the technology as a means for strengthening their work. This is what this book does by presenting documentation on a case study and a series of examples of 'better' uses. There is a broader purpose as well. This is to move beyond computer support to social action into the posing of questions regarding innovative effects that may be hidden or as yet not fully manifest in the use of the technology. An example already suggested is that computer-mediated communication supports non-hierarchical organization. Does CMC *induce* it? Is there something embedded in the history of the technology itself that may help in answering such questions? So a purpose here is to look 'beyond' the obvious to meanings and implications. This requires tools. If nothing else, it is hoped that this study will present some tools for examining a very new field of human endeavour.

In the latter part of the nineteenth century, rapidly accelerating industrialization and a contraction of state activities regarding social welfare led to increasing associative social politics in many countries. Many influential popular movements arose – for example, the labour movement, the temperance, dissenter and farmer movements. Some of these movements and organizations were involved in educational and social issues. One strength of the associations was that they could be more responsive to societal changes than the state. Another was that they articulated non-marketable needs and responses in spheres of human activity that had not become commodities. By their very success many of these movements, along with other organized interest groups, were co-opted into corporativistiç power structures.

In the latter part of the twentieth century, rapidly accelerating informationalization is witnessing the emergence of a new wave of associational activity. Many associations are the result of a disenchantment with the statist organization of society. Others are a result of the downscaling of the welfare state. Others are more directly a response to the problems of planetary survival. In advanced industrial societies, the new associations are working in a historical situation of an emerging post-industrialism in which immaterial production is replacing material production. Some call this 'information society'. In the poorer countries of the South, the struggle for development and justice are central. There is a growing awareness that the separation into First and Third Worlds is artificial and that developments in one part of the world not only affect the other but the two parts depend upon one another. Several scholars have pointed out the growing importance of the growing global networks of citizen movements, perhaps even for some future form of global self-governance. Hazel Henderson puts it this way:

> The blossoming of citizen-based organizations as one of the most striking phenomena of the 20th century has been described by Elise Boulding as 'a major shift in the nature of the international system.'
>
> Citizen movements and people's associations cover the whole range of human concerns – from service clubs, churches, self-help, and spiritual groups to chambers of commerce and professional associations of teachers, doctors, farmers, scientists, musicians, and artists – all sharing some concern for human society that crosses national borders.
>
> Citizen movements, now global as well as national and local, are key drivers in changing societies. They constitute an evolving form of democratic governance, sometimes rivaling the influence of heads of state, generals, scientists, inventors, and multinational corporate executives.[4]

Bubbling grassroots movements for more democracy challenging global elites has hardly gone unnoticed by these elites. The problem of 'governing democracy' has been the concern of the Trilateral

Commission, the Bilderbergers and others. And intellectuals such as Noam Chomsky and others on an individual and group basis have been watchdogging and criticizing these elites.

In his article *Computer Networks and the Emergence of Global Civil Society,* Howard Frederick argues that the new technology is being used for strengthening global civil society.

> The continued growth and influence of global civil society face two fundamental problems: increasing monopolization of global information and communication by transnational corporations; and the increasing disparities between the world's info-rich and info-poor populations. Global computer networking makes an electronic 'end-run' around the first problem and provides an appropriate technological solution to overcome the second.[5]

What is 'civil society'? A starting point here is the assumption that there are several different spheres of human activity and that each of these spheres has a different understanding of rationality and meaningful action. One sphere is private – that of home and family. Almost by definition, this sphere is closed from public scrutiny. The history of modern society is the story of an expanding public and democracy as an expanding citizenship. An ever-increasing share of human life comes under public scrutiny. People talk with more people about more things. This is, of course, a reflection of the socialization of material production: a basic definition of modern society is the social interdependence of individuals to survive.

The association developed between the family and the market and between the family and the state as a sphere of social activity. Many view this area of associative activity as the true civil society. This definition is less broad than the one in which civil society is everything outside the state sphere. But it is more precise and more analytically fruitful than one that includes both family and market. 'Civil society as association' deals, at least in part, with immaterial values and non-marketable spheres of human activity. But this definition of civil society is still very broad and it would be easy to discern other rationalities defining other spheres of human activity. Religion is a way of thinking (and living) that may be the strongest. Other rationalities and spheres of life are the aesthetical and the playful, just to mention two more. The point being made is an argument against reductionism. One way of obtaining some analytical order in the midst of a multiplicity of rationalities is to regulate some spheres to a position of subservience under state and market. Phenomena such as religion completely fall out of the contemporary Western intellectual frame of reference to such an extent that religiously motivated movements become nearly unintelligible.[6]

The purpose of this brief discussion of the different areas, or sectors, of family, state, market and association is to present an important starting point and perspective of this study: that these sectors comprise different cultures with different value systems and codes of behaviour. The *prime facie* validity of this assumption becomes apparent when boundaries are crossed from one system to another, for example trying to apply the rationality of one culture in another culture. Were I to run my family on a business-like, cost–benefit basis, I would rightly be accused of emotional disturbance and sent off to a psychoanalyst. When politicians start buying and selling power and influence in a businesslike fashion, we say they are corrupt. When businesspeople start doing something for nothing, we put them out of business. When associations start behaving like government agencies, we say they are co-opted or have become clients of the state.

The Promise and Threat of Information Technology

There is a growing body of literature that gives the digital revolution critical analysis. Many books have been written describing both the potential of '1984' society to become political reality thanks to modern electronics and the possible counter-usage of the same technology.

In the 1960s, Marshall McLuhan started writing about the long-term and subtle effects of the new electronic media on human culture and ways of perceiving the world. His telegraphic message 'the medium is the message' became accepted by many as a piece of proverbial wisdom. From his platform as international guru of mediology, McLuhan started talking about the future 'global village'. Again, this term has gained proverbial status. It denotes a situation in which every corner of the globe is reached – and penetrated – by the new media: radio, television, satellite-transmitted communications. Wars and revolutions are enacted 'live' in our living rooms, giving us, among other things, a sense of collapsing geography and history as a spectator sport. Obviously, the new media are a powerful tool: for power and control, for making money, or even possibly for liberation.[7] In his book *being digital* MIT professor Nicholas Negroponte pushes the argument forward, into the era of computer revolution. Information and communication technology is changing the way in which we live, and how we can interact with our surroundings, including other people.[8]

There are several critical theoretical frameworks within which communications research can be conducted.[9] One approach is a combination of symbolic interactionism, as first presented by John Dewey and expanded by others, and ideas around an expanding public sphere, the nature of communication in this sphere and the relation of public to private, as formulated by philosophers such as Jürgen Habermas.[10] The reason for this combination is the central common imperative: the development of the preconditions for participatory democracy. In Dewey's work a major focus is on developing socio-educational structures within the framework of modernity. Habermas is interested in the remodernization of modernity so as to develop systems of free discourse necessary for the maintenance of civil society and democracy.

One variant of the social interactionist approach to the study of the politics of information technology has its roots in political cconomy. The consequences of an emerging informational society take us back to basic political theory. This is because control over the new media is so clearly a function of political power. As Harold Lasswell pointed out in 1971, 'information without commitment leads to elitist bureaucracy.'[11] In 1986, Sean MacBride, who chaired a UNESCO commission on communication and society, called for a critique and examination of the ways in which information and communication affect 'the global economy, the distribution of political power, the growing gap between rich and poor and the relationship between multinational companies and national sovereign governments.'[12]

This is akin to the conceptual framework provided by a variant of structuralism: dependency theory.[13] The political economy of global information is seen as structured in patterns of centre–periphery relationships. The 'centre' is composed of the technologically advanced and economically dominant interests in the industrialized West. This 'centre' regulates the rest of the world to a peripheral position. There is, however, a 'periphery' in the 'centre' and a 'centre' in the 'periphery'. The structural dependency model sees the divisions in the world not solely in the geopolitical terms of First, Second and Third Worlds, or North/South, but in more differentiated patterns of dependencies and alliances. The pattern of relationships presented in dependency theory needs to be complemented with material and theoretical understanding of the role of international bodies, of both inter-state and non-governmental organizations (NGOs), and of multinational corporations. Various combinations and coalitions are possible between these actors. This study can be seen as a contribution to the growing body of knowledge concerning non-governmental organizations and ICT.

The technology

Technology is the interaction between people and machines. 'Information technology' is, then, the application of technology for dealing with the production, storage and distribution of information. Increasingly information technology is being based on the use of computers. In a review of futurist books on information technology one Swedish author saw the following scenario:

> In the 1960s the computer was seen as a mathematics machine. In the 1970s it became a word-processor and in the 1980s an instrument for desktop publishing. In the future the computer will be primarily an instrument for the distribution of an unlimited amount of information. Everyone will be able to reach everyone, anywhere – a scenario with almost inconceivable consequences.[14]

Many futurist writings explore the explosive developments taking place in the field of computer communications. Electronic media sometimes fall under the more general term 'information technology' to emphasize the relation and attachment to what is assumed to be an emerging 'information society'.[15] Enthusiasm over the new technology needs to be tempered by two serious considerations, however. The first is the fact of saturation: the amount of information that becomes available, or is pushed on an individual, can become insurmountable. The solution to this is the development of systems and people who can deal with and organize large quantities of information in meaningful ways. The other problem is that the new information technology is not available for all. Technological and above all economic hurdles are raised that prohibit democratic

What is 'computer-mediated communication'?

Computers can be connected to one another for exchanging information and sharing resources. In the 1960s and early 1970s, the US Department of Defense and a number of research universities started linking their computers to one another. The result was a network called ARPANET. The purpose was for sharing research and for communication. Electronic messages could be sent to other computers and to specific users on other computers. This is email and started as an electronic substitute for paper mail. This soon became so useful that other networks started appearing, mainly for those in academic work and for business purposes.

The interacting computers can be connected directly by cables, down the hall or around the globe. This is what banks and airlines do. This is obviously expensive if the computers are far apart. A cheaper way to do this is to use the cables already there, or to share a common cable with other computers – the telephone lines and the public cable networks for data transfer.

What is needed between an individual computer and the telephone line is a modem, which MOdulates and DEModulates digital signals from the computer to analogue ones used on the phone lines. Two computers equipped with modems can call each other and make an exchange. This can be automated. If dedicated cables are used then modems can be excluded.

When many people wanted to communicate with one another through their computers, at different times, a new way of doing this was developed. A common computer was set up, sort of an exchange that stored messages. Each user has a 'mailbox' for his or her 'electronic mail'. Hence the name 'mailbox systems'.

Users of email soon started sending copies of their messages to lists of people, known and unknown, in the hope that the receiver would be interested in reading what was written. Addressees soon found themselves drowned in email. To deal with this overload, 'conferencing' was developed. Messages are posted according to content and are stored and indexed together according to content. These 'content mailboxes' are known as 'conferences' on some systems, 'bulletin boards' or 'news groups' on others. It was now up to the reader to decide what he or she wanted to read. This was

---

a first step in the ongoing process in CMC systems of organizing information according to function, content and constituency.

Calling to a mailbox far away can be expensive. Keeping user costs down is a major impetus in the development of CMC systems, which, when interconnected to one another, form *networks*. Sometimes systems develop in which there is not one main computer, but several. Each computer in such a 'distributed' system is a mirroring of the information in the others, but with the possibility for local variations.

Information and Communications Technology, or **ICT** is another term used to denote the new technology. This term puts a little more emphasis on the distribution of information.

---

participation in the new global information system. This is the problem of access. For however one counts the access to computers and the World Wide Web and however fast the number of users seems to grow, the overwhelming majority of people with access to the new technology are in the North, whereas the overwhelming majority of people who inhabit this planet live in the South.

A new world information order?

Information is a commodity with an increasing market in post-industrial society. Yet information is also a social good since well-informed citizens are the basis of democracy. There is a potential conflict here since commodified information, for sale in the market, reduces citizenship to consumerism. Information is also a function of power: the major uses of information technology are commercial, industrial, military and for control purposes. As in all major technical revolutions, there are social and political implications. A major counter-trend, opposed to commodification, sees information as a social good and stresses the issues of content and communications development, available to all. This position was put forward by the Non-Aligned Movement and UNESCO, expressing itself as demands for a 'New International Information Order' (NIIO), and later as a 'New World Information and Communication Order' (NWICO).

The debate over the control of information and communication was intense in the 1970s and 1980s, leading to the withdrawal of the USA and the UK from UNESCO. The Anglo-American position was that the free flow of information had to be maintained and that it is the responsibility of governments and inter-governmental agencies to maintain this freedom. The position taken by Third World countries, backed by the socialist bloc, was that information and communication industries had a social responsibility in the process of development. The free-flow/open market position, as defined by the wealthy West, was seen as a continuation of colonialism and a widening of the information gap.

The course of events seemed to lead to a stalemate in the work of developing a strategy for a New World Information and Communication Order. The international political debate on this issue seemed to ebb for some years.[16] The reasons for this are not entirely clear. One reason may be that the battle of telecommunications is primarily between the USA, Japan and the European Community.[17] Another is that with only one superpower left, the TINA (There Is No Alternative) principle gained wide acceptance. However, the work of the MacBride Commission has been carried on, for example in the annual meetings of the MacBride Roundtable on Communication. Earlier the actors demanding an NWICO were state and inter-state agencies. New actors have taken up the task through creating alternative and community media on a global basis.

More of the same?

Is there an 'information and communications revolution'? Some say yes, and point to the exponential growth of the information and communications industries, the number of people working in information-related positions, the increasing reliance of business, industry and government on information processing, and so on. Others point to the fact that the new technology has been developed by and is in the hands of those already in powerful positions. In his book *The Network Revolution, Confessions of a Computer Scientist* (1982), Jacques Vallée writes that this is an example of a technology in search of an application. In other words, the 'information revolution' is an outgrowth of late capitalist production processes.[18] This argument has been expanded in a body of literature with catchy titles, such as

Silicon Snake Oil, written by Clifford Stoll in 1995. There is a growing body of 'backlash' literature that criticizes what are seen as attempts to technify more and more of every sphere of life. An example is Mark Slouka's *War of the Worlds – Cyberspace and the High-tech Assault on Reality* also published in 1995.

There is ample evidence that the politics of information technology is a mirroring and replication of conflicts found elsewhere. The North–South conflict over a new world order of information technology is a prime example. So, too, the intensifying competition between transnational corporations over technologies and markets, sometimes with support from national states. The shadow of trade war and protective legislation is ever present. It should be expected that the politics of information technology will reflect existing conflicts and tendencies within civil society: different organizations and movements have different ideas about how to make the world a better place, or keep it like it is. And we should expect other actors, such as states and businesses, to try to use, influence and even control the politics of information technology within civil society.

One variation on the theme of sameness is that *information is good business*. The spread of information technology means more consumers and more markets for both the hardware and the content. One does not have to be much of a Marxist to see that there is a very strong tendency toward monopolization. One critic alert to these tendencies is Ben H. Bagdikian, who has followed the monopolization of the media (from a North American perspective) since 1983, when the first edition of his book *The Media Monopoly* was published.[19] In his seminal study 'Lords of the Global Village', he punctured the cosiness of the global village metaphor.[20] Like in a real village in India, eastern Brazil or Harlan County, Kentucky, the lords control our livelihood by telling us what to eat, how to live, what to read and see, what to want and what to think.

The rapid growth of the Internet since 1994 in its commercialized and most visible application, the World Wide Web, has raised the hopes of many businesspeople that the email-order catalogue will be an economic panacea. And with audio and video on demand, media products can be WWW distributed and re-sold. All this requires bandwidth, a delivery system that provides the necessary infrastructure. This costs money. And people selling over the WWW are naturally interested in those with the economic resources to buy their products. This means a concentration of ICT to the North and to consumer segments in the North. So it is not surprising that some have found that the WWW has increased the 'information gap' between the North and the South.[21] Whether all this information is worth having is another question.

Those who see information technology as the midwife of 'a new industrial revolution' realize that information society requires an information technology infrastructure. Some strategic decisions have been made, others are pending. An often used analogy illustrates the situation. When automobiles started coming into use, demands were put on government for infrastructure investment in highways. This enabled the 'auto-mobilization' of the economy. Many government information technology policies have been like investing in traffic signs, driver education and the production of a specific car model. These policies increase the necessity for 'good digital highways'.

An example of this type of thinking on informational infrastructure is that of (then) US Senator Al Gore. In an effort to ensure US leadership in the global electronic village, he proposed that more be done in terms of education and infrastructure investment, for example in a fibre-optic network. To this end, he proposed legislation in the US Congress.[22] This snowballed, developing into plans for major investments in the 'InfoBahn' – the information superhighway of the future. This is intended to provide the informational infrastructure necessary to propel the United States into a position of world leadership in the use and development of 'information society'. The National Information Initiative (NII) has expanded into the global-ization of the information infrastructure. One organization working in this direction is the Global Information Infrastructure Commis-sion (GIIC), linked to global elites such as the G-8. The goal is explicit: to make certain that the North maintains its informational dominance and control over the South.

This is connected to another theme, arising out of the realization that *information technology requires strategic capitalist planning*. This issue is addressed by the MIT information technology think-tank volume *Technology 2001: The Future of Computing and Communications*. This book contains excellent futurology and competent analysis of what is happening on the cutting edge of the computing industry, including many problems, promises and dangers. Innovation in the new infor-mation technology occurs rapidly and is changing the world in which we are living and working. Our thinking and behaviour must change, and is changing. Why? Here this book is quite clear: to maintain the hegemony of the USA in the world.[23]

Another variation on the theme deals with possible opportunities and effects on democratic politics. This issue is addressed in the book *The Electronic Commonwealth: The Impact of New Media Technologies on Democratic Politics*. Under the aegis of the Harvard Institute of Politics, several leading political scientists and commentators analyse the impact of 'new media' on the political process. The problem is stated in a very clear-sighted way: used unwisely, the new media will worsen the problems of democracy; used wisely, the new media may open a door for a better type of democracy. This 'better' type is a communitarian form of democracy, with more citizens' participation – in contrast to the plebiscitary democracy of today, in which citizens are requested to acquiesce to the choices of competing elites. This brief sketch can hardly give due credit to this important statement of democratic concern regarding the new media and the future of democracy.

The search for and examination of experiments with what I have called 'better' uses of information technology is usually cast within a statist conceptual framework. Interest is directed toward several (not very successful) attempts at 'electronic town meetings' and 'citizen/decision-maker' electronic dialogues. In other words, the frame of mind is one of the technologization of the existing polity. The purpose of this is both clear and commendable: finding ways of dealing with a crumbling sense of common good (community) and a lurking crisis of legitimacy for the political process. The limitation of the statist conceptual framework then becomes clear: the study halts when it comes to an examination of uses of information technology in the non-state, non-business sector. The reason for this seems to be a distaste for or fear of a strengthened 'interest group' politics, sometimes called pluralistic democracy. The normative assumption made here is instead that the sought-for sense of the common good is not something that states create. Indeed, there is strong evidence that state power can be and is often used to the opposite end. The argument here is that community is created by the community – that is, not so much by 'citizens' working in a state structure but by what Vaclav Havel has called ethically responsible human beings working in society. This argument is of course prepositional, being a call for a study of civil society in terms not delimited by the necessarily power-oriented nomenclature of statist conceptualization.

Or seeds of social change?

A perennial question in the history of science, in history, and in the study of social and political change is the relationship of technology to change. Does new technology induce social change? Or is it the other way around: is it social changes that bring about new technologies? The question can obviously not be put in such simplistic terms. Instead, one needs to ask about the interrelationships between technology and social change, proceeding in an exploratory manner. It has been suggested above that there are a number of different ways of thinking about information and communication technology. By 'ways of thinking' is meant our perceptions of the technology, our fears, hopes and arguments for and against. Behind all this are numerous theories, or at least theoretical treatments that try to connect and interpret the new technology both to what we already know, or think we know, and to extrapolate into what might come about due to the new technology.

The different ways of thinking about information technology can be categorized in the following way: *the post-industrialists*, who see information society as both inevitable and qualitatively different from industrial society; *the telematic utopians*, who look to positive developmental effects of a widened communicative praxis; *the neo-liberal expansionists*, who see the exponential growth of the electronics and informatics industry as a promising new economic area; *the telematic sceptics*, who, in reaction to the former view, see information technology as a continuation and strengthening of commercial capitalism; *the information theorists*, who see information society in terms of the increasing complexity of modern life; and *the social constructionists*, who see technologies as socially and politically shaped.[24] Whatever the analytical arguments may be, there is more than ample evidence that many policy-makers, both public and private, *believe* that access to and control over information and its transmission is important.

It appears that the first generation of theorists of the information age have stated their cases. Research on information society has been moving for some time toward the development of sets of immediate theorization. This makes empirical studies easier and more meaningful. This is perhaps very natural: it is first when a technology becomes widespread and known that empirical studies of its uses can be done and reflected upon. What this means is that 'theory' on information technology and society will tend to become less and less unitary, with a number of separate discourses being conducted simultaneously. One of these will be explored below.

A broad summary of the impact of information and communication technology on society is presented by Manuel Castells in *The Information Age: Economy, Society and Culture*. His three volumes present both a synthesis of earlier discourse and a starting point for more specific inquiry. His perspective is that the new technology is affecting society very deeply. Control over the new modes of information is a question of power. While a main arena for politics is the media, and increasingly the new ICT media, there is very little political accountability here.[25]

'Informationalism', as concept and phenomenon, can be put on par with 'industrialism'. By informationalism is meant that knowledge, its production and dissemination, has become the dominant mode of production. Knowledge production replaces the production of goods and services as the ordering principle of society, the economy and culture. Castells' interest is in examining how the displacement of industrialism by informationalism is manifesting itself and what this might mean. A very visible form for this is the rise of ICT as an economic and social phenomenon. Informationalism compels the individual to reorient him/herself and re-examine social relationships, since these relationships are being redefined externally in what he calls 'the network society'. While most in the world are not 'online', all are being compelled to relate to the phenomenon of ICT and global electronic penetration. The age of the mass audience may be coming to an end. Does this mean the end of mass movements as well? What does it mean to become a global 'netizen', interacting more with others around the world than around the block?

Proceeding from 'informationalism' as a fruitful, ordering concept, the question arises of what kind of politics are emerging in the networked society, economy and culture? While it is surely too early for definitive answers, this study aspires to present some examples of a new type of political action and point to some relevant questions.

One discourse that has emerged out of earlier thinking on a projected information society, social theory and an increasing praxis of computer-mediated communication is around the question of *community*. Social theorists such as Robert Putnam and Amitai Etzioni have studied the decline of community and sought ways of reconstructing what is seen as the core of civil society: common identities, obligations and purposes (see Chapter 2). When their ideas are put in the context of information and communication technology, the following concrete question is generated.

Are online, 'virtual' communities 'real'?

The question is posed against the real or imagined backdrop of the demise of the nation-state: globalized capital seems to be breaking free of the state. Is the nation-state also losing authority over its citizens, who may be redefining themselves in terms of subcultures, both regional and global? The questions are many, their number growing. This leads back again to the argument that what is required is the concrete study of praxis.

In two anthologies, Steven G. Jones has collected a score of studies that rotate around the question of community and computer-mediated communication.[26] He sees CMC as 'socially produced space'.

> CMC, of course, is not just a tool; it is at once technology, medium, and engine of social relations. It not only structures social relations, it is the space within which the relations occur and the tool that individuals use to enter that space.[27]

The term 'cyberspace' was coined by fiction writer William Gibson in order to try and capture the nature of a 'space' both real and illusory. These volumes discuss CMC and community from a sociological perspective, with the Chicago school as a point of reference, through a survey of recent research on CMC. However, in spite of a stated awareness of the dangers of imparting too much importance to machines, much of the research here is still treating CMC, the Internet and computer technology as an independent factor that will induce social change. A lasting contribution of the studies will probably be the attempts to break the analysis of community out of the paradigm of place, moving it toward metaphors of culture and social networks.

The question of virtual communities being, or becoming, real has been given wide publicity in North America through, *inter alia*, Howard Rheingold's books on the subject (see Chapter 2). In his *Technopoly – The Surrender of Culture to Technology*, Neil Postman has criticized the idea of virtual communities as being real human communities, basically because there is no obligation in online interchanges.[28] And, as many have pointed out, there are all too many opportunities to be anonymous.

In 'Civil Society, Political Economy, and the Internet', Harris Breslow concludes the second volume on a somewhat pessimistic note: society for him is not 'post-modern' but 'post-civil'. The suburbia which he projects on the world is not the dense milieu needed for the public sphere of civil society. Interaction on the Internet underscores the isolation and privatization of contemporary society.[29]

Several things should already be obvious from this brief discussion so far of community and computer-mediated communication. The first is that it is very North American. It is probably not true that the majority of the Western world is living the middle-class American suburban lifestyle; it is definitely not true of the majority of people on this planet. The second is that there is no consensus about what is meant by community, reflected in the fact that it is common to use a qualifier such as local, real, virtual, and so forth. Another is the underlying assumption about 'modernity': that it in some way means dissolving 'traditional' communities as a universal, worldwide phenomenon. As any number of my Indian colleagues point out: why not stick together in order to face the problems and complexities of 'modern' – that is, contemporary – life, instead of opting into atomistic life-patterns?

Another, not so obvious point is that the academics seem to find it hard to look at how CMC is actually being used by social movements – that is, the intentional communities that are, as a by-product of their respective and joint activities, reconstructing civil society. Another reflection is on the hope of a 'Mac-community'. In this author's knowledge and experience, there is no such thing as instant community, either virtual or real. There is no technical 'fix'. Community building takes time. And time, a common history, is perhaps a most important component of any community.

It is possible to argue that there are intentional communities: that is, people working together for a common purpose. If this is the case then it is reasonable to assume that these communities can also operate 'online'. Can they germinate in the virtual reality of cyberspace? This book will present examples that show this does happen. Whether these intentional communities will stand the test of time, only time can tell; likewise, whether or not they will give rise to a new politics. For this seems to be a reason for the interest in community-building: the assumption that politics rests on community, seen in the traditional categories of physical proximity and dense interaction. Can there be a politics based on something else?

Is there any evidence that the new information technology in the specific form of computer-mediated communication *is being used* to bring about change? If this is so, is this a reflection of its use by progressive groups as a strengthening tool or is there something in the new information technology itself that induces change? What is the nature and quality of the evidence that can be mustered to illuminate these questions?

In *Technologies of Freedom*, Ithial de Sola Pool argued that the new information technology *can* be used for bringing about social and political change.[30] In an optimistic article in *Foreign Policy* in 1991, Sheldon Annis argued that the new technology could give a voice to the poor.[31] This view can be challenged, of course, on rather solid ground. The failure of the non-aligned movement and UNESCO and allies in creating a New World Information and Communication Order and the seemingly triumphant march forward of transnational corporations, with the electronics industry carrying the banners, seems to leave little room for an information technology for the poor.

Others are pessimistic on other grounds as well. An example is a study done by Suzanne Iacono and Rob Kling, 'Computerization Movements and Tales of Technological Utopianism'. Their conclusion is that while progressive social movements may use computers and networks to improve their own work, there is no comprehensive computerization movement that can offer a humanistic alternative to the mainstream path of computerization. They fear that computerization will strengthen existing social, economic and political structures.[32] This study argues against this conclusion. The first observation is that the world is larger than the USA: networks, computers and the whole of 'information society' cannot be understood on less than a global basis. Since the nation-state no longer occupies centre-stage, an analysis of politics of information technology cannot be made in a statist framework. A second observation is that phenomena such as 'computerization' must be studied dialectically. It has already been pointed out that the new technology is a major arena for economic and political conflict in the world today. What happens here – and what does not happen – must be seen in terms of conflict, but seen in such a way that allows for transformations in the course of inter-action. A third observation is that a study of 'computer movements' must actually study the movements and what they are doing.[33]

Linda Harasim's 1993 anthology *Global Networks* argued that there definitely is a social component to CMC beyond work efficiency. However, the studies do not really probe into the social uses of CMC. The closest is Howard Frederick's contribution – hardly surpris-ing since he has been actively involved in constructing and working with a network (PeaceNet in the USA) geared toward social action.

New, non-commercial and non-governmental informational infra-structures have started developing. These alternative, citizens' systems represent the clearest statement for the view of information as a social good. This spread of information technology is an attempt to strengthen civil society by making networking as public dialogue faster, easier and more global.[34] Non-governmental organizations, movements and groups, while working on the fringes of political power structures, are attempting to bring about basic changes re-garding the environment, peace, human rights and an equitable dis-tribution of global resources.[35] An important question is if and how these new networks are offering a way out of the previous stalemate and if they can offer a way to diminish the information gap, provide relevant content and spread of communications technology, while simultaneously maintaining a free flow.

What is 'Better'?

The 'better use' of a technology is not just futurology or intention but a use with the effect of bringing about a better world. 'Better' is, of course, a matter of value. At the threshold of a new millennium, this 'better' deals with issues of planetary survival and human dig-nity. Even if this definition may seem radical to some, it is one being adopted by many a non-radical: the epigraph to this chapter is the proposed research platform for a branch of the definitely non-revolutionary American Political Science Association.[36]

This study will be carried out in what Karl Popper has called the context of discovery. This involves a qualitative search for variations in the phenomena of ICT and a terminology for its classification. The rapid and multifaceted growth of the Internet shows that experience is uncontrollable, especially concerning computer-mediated communication.

What is 'better'? The question, and hence the answers, can be at different levels of understanding, abstraction and hence theory. At a take-off level, 'better' might mean simply something like 'making peace instead of war' with the new ICT technology. Clearly 'better' is both a question of value, of comparison, and of moving from one position to another. 'Better' is, of course, not an analytical category, even though it may be a very relevant frame for human life and action. But it can be used as a heuristic point of departure for illustrating the relation of man and machine brought out so clearly in the rapid development and dispersion of the new technologies. It should be remembered that 'technology' denotes not just machines but the relationship of people to their machines. Put another way, technology is how we use the machines. In this use is a whole set of social knowledges, experiences, expectations, fears and projections.

One level of 'better' is the progressive use of ICT for furthering the issues of planetary survival by groups and movements involved in disarmament and peace, reconciliation, protecting the environment, human rights, sustainable development, global justice. This is 'better' in an organized sense, linked to conscious efforts to bring about social change from an ideological position. Much of this book has this perspective as a starting point in the presentation of examples of how ICT is being used.

There is another level of inquiry as well. This deals with the empowering effects of using ICT in better ways. Empowerment must be understood dialectically, in relation to the dis-empowerment in basic spheres of life due to globalized media, markets and control structures. This is a theme developed by Cees Hamelink in such works as his *World Communication – Disempowerment and Self-Empowerment*. For most, the global village penetration of mass media has meant disempowerment, in part through a redefinition of how the world 'is' and how it should be perceived. This is not only villagers in remote parts of India sitting in thatched huts looking at *Bay Watch* but also the accompanying commercialization and selection of what is newsworthy. World communication has been largely one-way, a form of electronic colonialization.[37]

Hamelink points out that an area for resistance to electronic colonialization (this author's term) may be available in the intersection between the global and the local, which does not disappear simply because it has been incorporated into a global structure. He suggests that there may be an alternative access and participation approach to empowerment. This might be based on technical assistance, of the kind provided by UNESCO and the UNDP. It might also take the form of 'people's media', for example through people's networks. Hamelink's working example is the Third World Network. The alternative might also mean the 'revolt of civil society' through a process of localization in opposition to globalization. These factors can, of course, work in tandem. An attempt at formulating a concise alternative to globalized media is found in the 'People's Communication Charter'.

The renewed attempt to put forward demands for a new information and communication order has not gone unchallenged. New regimes for controlling the new ICT in an emerging informationalism are appearing. Some are formalized in international treaties and organizations. A critical area of conflict is over intellectual property rights. Another is the perennial state drive toward censorship and northern penetration of the South.

One characteristic of the new technology (ICT) is that it is so uncontrollable. Danish philosopher Ole Thyssen has pointed out that this may be intrinsic. Historically speaking, a technology cannot control itself. Trains rushing down the rails cannot control themselves – that is, cannot coordinate their activities. It was when the telegraph was developed that timetables for trains first had any meaning. As yet, there is no technology that goes beyond ICT in the sense of being able to control its expansion in all directions.[38]

Getting to 'better'

A question that the emergence of ICT brings into sharp focus is that of the relation of action to information.[39] Information does not necessarily lead to action and lack of information does not necessarily lead to inaction. Yet in a complex world it is commonly accepted that at least one necessary condition for action is information. In an attempt to formulate the relationship between information and change, Ole Thyssen presents a cognitive scheme:

information → performation → innovation

Performation is a speech act that in the performance of utterance constitutes an action, such as the statement 'I am communicating with you.' When said, it is a piece of communication. In a social and private space increasingly filled and penetrated by information that is or purports to be other people's performations, the theatrical aspect increases. We are presented not with other individuals but with personae. The net causes us to reconsider selfhood.[40]

'Innovation' is probably best understood in terms of changed cognition and perceptions. In the 'over-crowded room of post-modernity', the info-push toward continuous innovation can, and has, gone off into 'virtual reality'. But it also creates new intersections, complementing and perhaps augmenting the free space in the crossing of global and local. An example here would be the inter-netted, postmodernistic writings of Subcommandante Marcos, one of the leaders of the Chiapas movement in Mexico (see Chapter 4).

Studying the Politics of Information Technology

A classic definition of 'politics' is 'who gets what', a definition that focuses attention on distribution as the core of this area of analytic – and human – endeavour. A variation of this, possibly with less materialist connotation, is that politics is 'the authoritative allocation of value'. These definitions point to both conflict and regulation. In this study, attention will be directed to the way different social forces are attempting to stake out claims in a new area of social endeavour – information technology. What, then, is 'politics'? The definition used here is one adapted from the study of social politics:

'Politics' can be said to occur when some group (or factor) in society attempts to change, or is changing, its place in society, in relation to another group or society itself. This change can be material or immaterial. This includes both perception, knowledge and power positioning.

This definition allows for the study of social movements and change in terms that do not necessarily commit 'politics' to the study of states, and the organization of society in statist categories. In other words, this is a post-statist definition. 'Power positioning' is not just a question of resources but also of the degrees of autonomy, external control and perceptions of these. It draws attention to the changing focus of legitimacy, and of social organization. In the networked society it may be that the individual relates mainly to his or her subculture and only through this subculture to a network of other subcultures, perhaps seen as the nation or the world.

Moving beyond statist definitions becomes relevant, for example, when analysing those organizations thrown together in the category 'NGO', non-governmental organization. This way of naming an organization or movement is regulatory: it immediately establishes the control of the state by defining the way in which we are to think. Many discussions of 'civil society' tend to operate within the statist paradigm. The definition of politics suggested here is an attempt to avoid this type of predetermination.

Information technology has its own politics beyond the invest-ment and distributive policies connected to the development of IT industry and infrastructure. The movement of more and more infor-mation, information exchange and retrieval, communications and transactions into global 'cyberspace' (the Internet, matrix, World Wide Web, etc.) is affecting the social system. Policies and policy-making processes are being redefined and are redefining themselves. A new, 'wired' political community is emerging, a *net-polis*. The contours and nature of this political community are only in formation, nebulous. The task of research is to study what is happening, why, and what possible patterns might emerge. A major concern – for politicians, scholars and citizens – is maintaining democratic values in cyber-space: equal access, responsibility, representativity, public control and accountability.[41]

The problem of democracy in cyberspace suggests several areas for research. One area deals with general theoretical issues. This is because IT is having an impact on the whole of society. Chris C. Demchák, writing in a newsletter of the American Political Science Association, puts it this way:

> The challenge for theory is to explain the processes by which the rela-tively innocent designs often based on local requirements can ultimately induce crucial changes in the society's internal and external interactions,

not to mention the values, goals and impedimenta of the social system. Often unrecognized in its influence, the IT design forces a configuration of the community's obligations, opportunities, resources, constraints, secrets and power. Advances in theory or concepts here must elegantly account for interactions within and between broad socially significant categories of phenomena and knowledge.[42]

A second area of study would deal more directly with the effect of ICT on the policy-making process. An example would be how the political agenda may be redefined when what is networked defines knowledge, problems and solutions. Another area deals with issues of organizational theory and public policies, for example how organizational structures, both public and private, are influenced by participation in cyberspace and how 'cyberorgs' (online organizations) influence public policy. Another area for research would deal with issues of individual experiences and possibilities for an emergent 'networked democracy'.[43]

The research strategy presented above is mainstream in its approach: the questioning is classical, although the phenomenon to be studied is new. This means that another area is impending, which attempts to extract new ways of conceptualization out of the emerging new *praxis* of cyberspace. This study examines one such area: how networking is being used for social and political change and networking as social and political change, including democratization.

When society is not experienced as unchangeable, but in a process of continual change, then the descriptions of the direction of change become highly normative. These pictures of the future illustrate what is empirically possible and normatively attractive. Theory and practice become tied to each other in the sense that utopias are projected and made, not as entire systems (which would demand a theoretical understanding of that which is not) but as *praxis*. This is both in terms of process and project. The core of utopia shifts from a state of affairs to process, from a place in the future to a movement toward a future. The normative element of emancipatory or utopian praxis is expressed in a theory of human rights. Understood dialectically, this means basic and intrinsic rights to both life and resistance to dehumanization. The (re)construction of civil society, outside the rationalities of commodification, state and capital, should be understood from the perspective of emancipatory praxis.

The emerging of a 'utopian' or 'better' praxis of a subset of information technology can be viewed and analysed in a fruitful way from the perspectives provided by Jürgen Habermas. One core of his critical approach to the understanding of society and modernity are the concepts of communicative action and public discourse. Whereas the former assumes that a communicated message contains elements of human intercourse, the latter demands a critical analysis of the message to find out whether human interaction is, in fact, occurring.[44] Proceeding from an interest in everyday language, Habermas seems to be saying that the plurality of rationalities in the life-world can (or must) have a common, universal base in communicative rationality. A central interest here is the issue of 'unrestricted dialogue'. CMC would seem to offer a technology for greatly expanding the public sphere of free communicative interaction that Habermas – and many others – consider a hallmark of modern society. Communication, as speech acts, can lead to understanding and perhaps something more. It is this 'perhaps' and 'something more' that has generated a growing academic and practical interest in CMC as a tool and catalyst for the (re)construction of civil society and community.

This way of approaching CMC as vehicle in the public sphere assumes, or preconditions, a meta-agreement that a rational solution can be reached (at least in principle). As we shall see later, many networked and interactive fora in citizens' networks seem to operate on the basis of such a meta-agreement. The rationality of discourse must be free. There must be a freedom from external control, for example from the hegemony of state and capital, and there must be a freedom of access to the means of communication and discourse. This study claims to be an exemplification of this idea, that an area of free discourse can be created and maintained, in the case at hand through the special adaptation of a new technology.

In the present world of many possible futures, control over consciousness of what these may be becomes central. When rebellions break out or coups are staged, it is no longer factories and railway stations that are the focus of the physical struggle, but television and radio stations, and, to a lesser degree, newspapers. Oppressive regimes find it as important to control journalists as armed insurgents in the hills. An important part of the strategic planning in situations of superpower intervention is controlling the flow of information.

In the first decades of the twentieth century, Antonio Gramsci began analysing the implications of the industrialization of culture and the appearance of an information industry. What he saw was that the 'mode of information' was beginning to replace the 'mode of production' as the underlying driving force of social change. He also understood first that when the mode of information became dominant it would be possible to think in the categories necessary for creating a theoretical understanding of 'information society'.

The neo-Gramscian theoretical tradition provides a starting point for grasping the social and political meaning of information technology. In his early analyses of the importance of the industrialization of culture, Gramsci developed the fruitful concept of hegemony ('early' here denotes his predating the work of the Frankfurt School.) The application of Gramsci's ideas is that the superstructure, to speak in Marxist terms, has an independent, even decisive, influence on the organization of the material base. The adaptation presented *inter alia* by Renate Holub emphasizes this.[45] In a historical situation in which the most dynamic economic element in 'advanced' – that is, rich – societies is shifting from material to immaterial production, the issue of control over the means of ideological and cultural hegemony becomes central.[46]

The neo-Gramscian hypothesis is that the importance of *the mode of production* is being superseded by *the mode of information*. Concretely, it is the shape, content and control over 'information' that determines both 'who gets what, where' and how we perceive and live our lives. This is especially true in a uni-polar world in which the one remaining superpower is striving for hegemony over the mode of information. The hypothesis appears to be fruitful since it can be applied at different levels: theoretically, in the manner suggested above; ethically, as done by the MacBride commission; and politically, for example the ongoing debate around 'World Trade Organization' – which promotes agreements on world trade in the field of telecommunications among others – and the penetration of information technology. This is why there is a growing interest in the study of the emerging control regimes, attempted and implemented by state and inter-state bodies.

This study is positioned in the intersection of ICT and civil society. It has been conducted within the framework of exploratory action research. This means that there is a good deal of hitherto unpublished documentation contained in the following pages. This is a warning to those careful academic readers who might get worried about too much detail. The specific purpose is to examine how the new technology is being used for positive social change. Is all this intentional or does the new technology induce changes in social interaction? This perennial question perhaps needs some serious rephrasing. And this task would lead us too far afield from the present study. If we see 'technology itself' as a sum total of many small intentionalities, then something is happening.

Where do the examples of computer support for social action come from? There are several sources. The first source is from the literature that has dealt with the projected possibilities for computer-mediated communication. This is the 'what if' literature of hopes for better uses for the new technology. A second, and major, source arises from the roots of the technology itself: that is, in the history of the PC revolution as an experiment in emancipatory social action. These roots point to where to start looking for applications of computer support for social action: among groups that are already involved in emancipatory social action. A third source of examples is from personal and collective experience within the community of communication activists. A fourth source is a case study of networking in a war zone in former Yugoslavia.

All these sources have generated examples and, out of these, a categorization pointing toward a typology of computer support for social action. This material, potentially a vast array of examples, is given a qualitative analysis with the intent of discovering some of the boundaries of such uses and social dynamics of the technology. The essence of this type of analysis is that the categories should cover the phenomenon and that each should be mutually exclusive and yet comprehensive enough to generate meaning.[47] A major task here is to generate a language for perceiving and analysing the new types of phenomena that ICT induces or may induce.

On a somewhat different methodological tangent: this book is a study in the process of performance. And this from the participant's perspective: the examples presented are 'information and communication actions' that the actors themselves believe to be part of or support for innovation and social change.

The use and development of ICT are interwoven. The way the 'computer revolution' has taken place has allowed certain types of uses. Conversely, these uses have shaped the development of ICT. In order to understand the concrete ways in which ICT has been used in historical situations, it is necessary to examine first how the technology emerged. This is the theme of the next chapter.

Notes

1. Swedish Radio, P1, Lunch Eko, 10 October 1997.
2. The term 'humanization' is used in the European and South American sense, not in the somewhat anti-clerical North American sense. More specifically I use the term in the same way that Paulo Freire uses it, as a struggle for liberation against dehumanizing conditions of ignorance, poverty and oppression.
3. This, along with many other ways of considering the 'utopian', is dealt with by the Danish philosopher Ole Thyssen in his *Utopisk dialektik* (Utopian Dialectics), Copenhagen 1976.
4. Hazel Henderson, 'Global Networks', originally in *IN CONTEXT*, no. 36, Fall 1993, also online at URL: <http://www.context.org/ICLIB/IC36/Hendersn.htm>.
5. Howard Frederick, 'Computer Networks and the Emergence of Global Civil Society: The Case of the Association for Progressive Communications (APC)', in Linda Harasim and Jan Walls, eds, *Globalizing Networks: Computers and International Communication*, Cambridge MA 1993.
6. This point was brought out to me recently by Ananta Giri, researcher at the Madras Institute of Development Studies.
7. One of Marshall McLuhan's classic works is *Understanding Media: The Extension of Man*, New York 1964.
8. Nicholas Negroponte, *being digital*, New York 1995.
9. 'Critical' refers here to post-positivitic research traditions. See Pradip Chakravarty and Sunita Vasudeva, 'Communications Research: One Paradigm or Plurality of Views? Taking Stock of a Discipline', in *Social Action*, April–June 1991, vol. 41, no. 2, pp. 176–95.
10. John Dewey, *Democracy and Education*, New York 1916; Jürgen Habermas, *The Theory of Communicative Action*, Cambridge 1984.
11. Alan F. Westin, ed., *Information Technology in a Democracy*, Cambridge 1971.
12. Michael Traber, ed., *The Myth of the Information Revolution – Social and Ethical Implications of Communication Technology*, London 1986; cf. the UNESCO commission findings, in Sean MacBride, *One World, Many Voices*, Paris 1980.
13. Johan Galtung, 'A Structural Theory of Imperialism', in I. Vogeler and A.R. DeSouza, eds, *Dialectics of Third World Development*, New York 1980.
14. 'Alla når alla med framtidens dator', *Svenska Dagbladet*, 11 February 1992; review of Derak Leebart, ed., *Technology 2001: The Future of Computing and Communications*, Cambridge MA 1991.

15. Since this field of study is new, the terminology falters and is sometimes lacking.
16. Howard H. Frederick, *Global Communication and International Relations*, Belmont CA 1997.
17. Gérard Longuet, 'The World Battle of Telecommunications', *Politique internationale* 34, Winter 1986–87, pp. 193–202.
18. Jacques Vallée, *The Network Revolution, Confessions of a Computer Scientist*, Berkeley 1982; published in Sweden under the title *Det osynliga nätet. En dataexperts bekännelser*, Stockholm 1984.
19. Ben H. Bagdikian, *The Media Monopoly*, 4th edn, Boston 1992.
20. Ben H. Bagdikian, 'Lords of the Global Village', *The Nation*, 12 June 1989.
21. See 'The Internet and the South: Superhighway or Dirt-track?', *The Panos Media Briefing*, no. 16, October 1995.
22. *Scientific American*, special issue, September 1991.
23. Stated quite clearly in the introduction, and elsewhere, in Derak Leebart, ed., *Technology 2001: The Future of Computing and Communications*, Cambridge MA 1991.
24. See Don Schiller, 'How to Think About Informatics', in Vincent Mosco and Janet Wasko, eds, *The Political Economy of Information*, Madison WI and London, 1988; Bent Madsen and Arne Mortensen, *Computermagt og menneskevaerd* (Computer Power and Human Value), Copenhagen 1985; Wiebe E. Bijker, Thomas P. Hughes and Trevor J. Pinch, *The Social Construction of Technological Systems: New Directions on the Sociology and History of Technology*, Cambridge MA 1987.
25. Manuel Castells, *The Information Age: Economy, Society and Culture*, 3 vols, Oxford 1997.
26. Steven G. Jones, ed., *CyberSociety – Computer-Mediated Communication and Community*, London 1995, and *Virtual Culture – Identity and Communication in Cybersociety*, London 1997.
27. Jones, ed., *CyberSociety*, p. 16.
28. Neil Postman, *Technopoly – The Surrender of Culture to Technology*, New York 1993.
29. Harris Breslow, 'Civil Society, Political Economy, and the Internet', in Jones, *Virtual Culture*, pp. 236–55.
30. Ithial de Sola Pool, *Technologies of Freedom*, Cambridge 1983.
31. Sheldon Annis, 'Giving Voice to the Poor', *Foreign Policy*, no. 84, Fall 1991, pp. 93–106.
32. Suzanne Iacono and Rob Kling, 'Computerization Movements and Tales of Technological Utopianism', in Rob Kling (ed.), *Computerization and Controversy: Value Conflicts and Social Choices*, 2nd edn, San Diego CA 1995.
33. Unfortunately, Iacono and Kling did not do this, completely missed the hacker/computer-lib movement, etc.

34. Mikael Böök, *Nätbyggaren: En undersökning av den moderna posten* (The Net-builder: A Survey of Modern Mail), Helsinki 1989.
35. Cees J. Hamelink, 'Global Communication: Plea for Civil Action', in B.V. Hofsten, ed., *Informatics in Food and Nutrition*, Stockholm 1991, pp. 5–8. See also 'Communication: The Most Violated Human Right', Inter-Press Service dispatch, 9 May 1991 (ips.news on APC).
36. Edward Woodhouse, 'New Section Project: The Political (Re)Construction of Technology', in *Science and Technology Studies Newsletter* (American Political Science Association), vol. 5, no. 1, December 1992.
37. Cees Hamelink, *World Communication – Disempowerment and Self-Empowerment*, London 1995.
38. This is a basic theme argued by Thyssen in several of his works, for example *Nutiden: Det overfyldte rum* (The Present: The Overcrowded Room), Copenhagen 1993.
39. Thanks to Fritz Florin, Culemburg, the Netherlands, for reminding me of this.
40. Cf. Thyssen, *Nutiden*, pp. 109 ff., and Castells, *The Information Age*.
41. Chris C. Demchák, 'Cyberspace and Emergent Body Politic', *Policy Currents*, vol. 4, no. 4/94, pp. 1, 6–9.
42. *Ibid.*, p. 6.
43. *Ibid.*
44. A summary of the theory is found in Habermas, *The Theory of Communicative Action*, ch. 3.
45. Renate Holub, *Antonio Gramsci: Beyond Marxism and Postmodernism*, London 1992.
46. A main bone of contention between the USA and western Europe in the concluding round of GATT negotiations (December 1993) was over immaterial production – the content of information technology.
47. Bo Eneroth, *Hur möter man vackert?* (How Do You Measure Beautiful?), Gothenburg 1989.

2
Going for IT

A starting point for this analysis is that it is meaningful to study the emancipatory uses of information technology. The social experiments studied here are not construed, or even planned. They are not laboratory cases, or publicly financed 'projects' under controlled conditions, but actual events and organizations serving real movements for social and political change. This means that these uses are difficult to monitor and categorize. This is especially true in a situation of dynamic expansion and change – in the words of many network builders, 'networking is spreading like wildfire', and even experienced network builders have difficulty in keeping abreast of what is happening.

A new technology does not just happen. It is created and introduced. The spread of computer technology, in the form of personal computers, and computer-mediated communication is a vivid example of this proposition. These two phenomena were not planned, or even wanted, spin-offs of high-end technology. The history of the development and spread of these technologies illustrates one meaning of 'better' use.

Computer Lib: Round I

The technology, developed by the military and large corporations and used in the academic world, depends on 'leased lines' – physical cables used solely (dedicated) for data transfer. These are expensive and someone has to pay, the someone being either the taxpayer or the consumer of corporate products and services. This technology has also depended on large, centrally placed computers known as 'mainframes'. Individual users were connected to the mainframe through their terminals. This technology was presented as The Technology, something understood by the few and in the hands of the still fewer. This attitude aroused the fears of many and the literature of the period abounds in works of warning about the dangers of the new information technology. These warnings were not only, or even primarily, technological so much as political fears of the technology winding up solely in the hands of the already powerful. These fears were fuelled by the fact that through the 1970s the politics of information technology was restrictive.

Through the 1960s, and into the 1970s, IBM was the overshadowing actor on the computer market. The technology was geared to big customers and compact, inexpensive computers for the general public were not part of IBM's strategy at that time, though this was technically possible.[1] This left room for others to enter. The 'others', described by Steven Levy in his collective biography *Hackers: Heroes of the Computer Revolution,* were several sets of young computer enthusiasts. One first group had its roots in MIT's computer laboratory in Cambridge, Massachusetts. Fighting their way to access the state-of-the-art computers of the time – gigantic machines that batch-processed cards and paper tape – these first hackers broke ground in developing ways to do interactive computing. Probably more important than the technical advances made was the formulation of what Levy calls 'the Hacker Ethic'. This was a new way of looking at machines, a new relationship between people and computers – that is, a new 'technology'.

The Hacker Ethic was first and foremost a hands-on approach to computing. Instead of first theorizing about what could or could not be done before implementing, the hackers set about doing it, fixing ('debugging') errors along the way. The term 'hack' refers in the new language of computerese to this way of doing things. Hacking a solution means sticking to a task until it works, jumping around barriers, if need be with wire and soldering iron. A 'good hack' is the simplest and aesthetically most pleasing solution to a problem. Thus the Hacker Ethic was intensely anti-bureaucratic and against hierarchical social organization. You were judged by what you could do, not your social rank, or age (many hackers were high school kids). Partly as a reaction to the secretive, white-robed priesthood of computer science, the Hacker Ethic proclaimed that information wanted to be free – including computer codes. All tools for computing should be available to everyone and locked doors were there to be cracked open – not for profit, but just because the art and science of computing could not develop in a closed environment. This attitude of openness went hand in hand with a fun-and-games approach that soon developed its own aesthetics. This was the flip side of strict computer logic and perhaps a creative necessity for finding new solutions. It also was a critique of the dominant utilitarian approach to computing. The early hackers had a hard time conceiving of computing for profit. They wanted the power of the computer. Having fun with computers was justification enough; a new 'life space' was opening up. The Hacker Ethic was thus very anarchistic, and it is not just this author who, as a project leader, has discovered that trying to get computer hackers to follow an organizational plan or time chart is like trying to herd cats.

Steven Levy, like this author, uses the term 'hacker' in its original meaning rooted in computer pioneering. In this usage, the connotations are positive: free spirits breaking down barriers to knowledge. However, because of many cases of misuse of the unleashed power of personal computing, the term became tarnished, even discredited. The hacker became either a 'nerd', a social recluse, or a 'cracker', a criminal hacker. A whole literature developed around this. But there is a solid argument, as presented below, for retaining the term 'hacker' in its original, historical sense.[2]

While the East Coast software hackers described above maintained a certain elitism, it was in California that the egalitarian hardware hackers flourished. This important group is described by Theodore Roszak in the following way:

> But by the end of the 1960s, there was another species of hackers on the horizon, emerging mainly on the West Coast [of the USA] from the ranks of the antiwar movement. These were the radical or guerrilla hackers, who were destined to give the computer a dramatically new image and a political orientation it could never have gained from Big Blue [i.e. IBM] or any of its vassals in the mainstream of the industry. At their hands, information technology would make its closest approach to becoming an instrument of democratic politics.[3]

One early meeting of socially concerned hackers, with involvement in the Vietnam war protest movement, took place in the spring of 1970 at the University of California in Berkeley.

They deplored the fact that the computer was being monopolized for profit and power by the same military–industrial complex that already controlled every other major technology. Yet they were also convinced that their profession held the key to a vital participatory democracy. That key was information.[4]

The ideological, social and even technological roots of the development of the personal computer, which enables decentralized computer-mediated communications, thus go back to the Berkeley free speech and anti-war movements of the 1960s. The search for, and development of, a 'people's information technology' provided a powerful impetus for later developments.

Several community-oriented projects and social experiments were started. Out of 'Resource One', a community data base, a project called 'Community Memory' emerged in the Bay Area. This was an electronic bulletin board. While these early experiments were local and still tied to existing, mainframe technology, they were proving a point: that information, and information in electronic form, could be much more than an industrial or commercial commodity. Breaking out of the existing technology was the next step.

> From its beginning, the microcomputer was surrounded by an aura of vulgarity and radicalism that contrasted sharply with the mandarin pretensions of the high tech mainstream. This is because so much of the new, smaller-scaled technology was left to be developed outside the corporate citadel by brash young hackers – especially in California, where socially divergent types had gathered along that strip of the San Francisco peninsula which was coming to be called Silicon Valley. By the mid-1970s, small groups of these hackers had begun to meet in informal rap sessions where computer lore was freely swapped like gossip over the cracker barrel in a country store. The feel of these meetings was deliberately down-home: a self-conscious rejection of the stilted corporate style.[5]

One of the most colourful and productive of these 'funky town meetings' was the Homebrew Computer Club in Menlo Park, near the Stanford University campus. Much of what took place there has become legend in the folklore of the cybernetic revolution. It was at Homebrew that Stephen Wozniak, together with Steven Jobs, presented his new microcomputer in 1977: the Apple. Two years before this, several hackers in Albuquerque had started circulating the first microcomputer, a mail order kit named the Altair (after an alien planet in the *Star Trek* television series). The Altair, backed by the

Whole Earth Catalog, became a success and harbinger of things to come, and was from the start perceived as a technology of liberation.[6]

The West Coast group is what Steven Levy calls the 'hardware hackers' – people who were actually building new machines and using the type of interactive software developed by the first generation of hackers at MIT. He also chronicles the emergence of a third generation, the 'game hackers'. The aspect of fun had always been part of the hacker culture and 'getting the machine to do something' seems to have been easily conceptualized and implemented in the form of games. These were either arcade games imported into PCs or 'Star Wars' and/or 'adventures' played on PCs, mainframes and around the Net. That recreational computing would have such an appeal perhaps surprised many – but again, the corporations and academic world were both tardy in presenting 'useful' applications for personal computing. The phenomenon is witness to the holding power of the technology and to the strong appeal of gaining access to a 'free space', a place devoid of regulation, including the control of utilitarian demands of the workplace and social responsibility. In other disciplines this is known as 'play', something children are seen to need to do in order to learn and grow but sorely out of place in the world of adults who are denied this life-space.

To paraphrase Walter Benjamin, secularized societies based solely on money have to construct ways of interpreting existential experience. The vast popularity of the televized fairy tales known as soap operas support his observation – as does the spread of certain types of computer games. It is perhaps in the sense of being in control that is a major component in the holding power of the computer. Novelty obviously has its own attraction but so does the sense (true or false) of personal empowerment. Computer games provide escape and entertainment, sometimes something more. Through symbolic representations of the world and through the power of narrative and fairy tale, the computer-game culture provides avenues of interpretation for both understanding and manipulating experiences in symbolic form. As Bruno Bettelheim has pointed out, going through the trials and tribulations, constantly making choices, usually between good and evil, is the essence of the fairy tale. There is great interpretive and therapeutic power here, for both children and adults.[7]

In this adventure game subculture, there is a strong presence of Tolkien. Some of the earlier 'dungeons and dragons' adventure games broke out of the confines of the machine, developing into person-to-person, interactive 'live' theatre.[8] The interactiveness of computer adventure games enhances the feeling of being in control, not of reality of course, but of the experience and interpretation of reality, with alternative outcomes and perhaps a heightened sense of possible meanings. Meaning needs company. When it later became technically and economically feasible to create a multi-user dimension (MUD), the adventure games quickly picked up on this. Like solving riddles, these can also be intellectually stimulating. So it is not surprising to find that rather sophisticated simulation software applications are packaged as games.

The game hackers soon discovered that there was a very large market for their software, as did many of the hardware hackers. Some arrived on this new technological frontier with dollar signs in their eyes and went straight for the goldmines. New companies were set up that produced new machines and software for them, forcing the big computer corporations to take the PC revolution seriously. Stewart Brand, founder of the *Whole Earth Catalog*, put it this way:

> I think that hackers – dedicated, innovative, irreverent computer pro-grammers – are the most interesting and effective body of intellectuals since the framers of the U.S. Constitution.... No other group that I know of has set out to liberate a technology and succeeded. They not only did so against the active disinterest of corporate America, their success forced corporate America to adopt their style in the end. In reorganizing the Information Age around the individual, via personal computers, the hack-ers may well have saved the American economy.... The quietest of all the '60s subcultures has emerged as the most innovative and powerful.[9]

In the early days of the microcomputer (and perhaps even today) most enthusiasts were not quite clear why they wanted this powerful piece of technology. ('Recipes for quiche?' 'Cataloging records?') In hindsight, however, it is clear that the emphasis was on 'powerful': wresting at least part of this technology from the military–industrial complex was an act of empowerment, not unlike learning to read and write, or perhaps even the right to vote. In the words of Lee Felsen-stein, a pioneer of Homebrew and the microcomputer revolution,

> They just wanted to get their hands on the technology and control it from below. In 1978 personal computers found their first big function: communication. Alan Kay had been saying for years that a computer was

first, second and thirdly a communications tool. Ward Christensen and Randy Seuss opened a BBS in Chicago in February of that year, and the rest is history. The number of BBS systems is unknown and probably unknowable. All this in spite of primitive software technology.... This was indeed a demand-driven application, and it is important to note that the demand was not for official, certified, top-down information, but for contact with other people having kindred interests.[10]

What Ward Christensen had developed was a protocol that allowed for error-free transfer of data over a modem and telephone line. This was another step in 'capturing the technology' from the corporations, the military and academic networks who were (and still are) operating on platforms of leased lines. The difference may at first glance seem a mere technical difference but the argument being put forward here is that this is of crucial social and political significance. The democratization of the technology has meant increasing access. 'Access' means availability to citizens both in a technological and economic sense: cost and ease of use; and, of course, that the technology is there, physically, and that there is some meaning to its use. A technology that is too expensive has limited access. Likewise, if it is too difficult to use, it will not be used. If it has no meaning, it will be seen as irrelevant.

Running off newly available PCs and modems, countless Bulletin Board Systems (BBSes) started appearing. More often than not, these were run by amateur hackers, fascinated by the new technology. Much of the content was 'introvert' in the sense that it dealt with the technology itself: exchanging computer programs and ideas on computing (plus a lot of nonsense). But out of this BBS culture of interaction developed many things of lasting importance. One was cost-consciousness and anti-commercialism. Since the BBS hackers were paying their own way, ingenious ways of cutting costs emerged. FidoNet is one; the development of a culture of public domain (no cost) and shareware (use first, pay later) software is another.

Running a BBS means running a piece of software that will answer the phone when a user (i.e. the user's computer) calls in and provide some services: exchange of mail, information in other forms, program swapping. This is what a stand-alone BBS does. But most BBSes go beyond this since the bottom line has been to save money. So a BBS in one place exchanges mail and other material with another BBS in another place. In this way, a user only has to dial in to the closest BBS, saving long-distance phone costs. Much like the amateur short-wave relay networks in the earlier part of the century, a BBS network known as FidoNet developed. The basic principle of the FidoNet is that a BBS need only make a relatively short-distance call to another nearby BBS to exchange material to and from nearly any place around the world. Since telephone cost is not only distance but time as well, some sophisticated programming has come out of the BBS culture, as well as providing both a market and impetus for the development of high-speed modems.

The hacker/BBS culture is non-commercial, at times aggressively anti-commercial. The best expression of this is the development of public domain and shareware software. This culture has always been critical of the high pricing of computer software. Many feel that this pricing sets up barriers to access to information technology. Some might argue that no one should 'own' the intellectual property basic to basic democratic (electronic) communication – like trying to patent the English language. Many programmers develop their software as 'shareware'. This means that the software is distributed free of cost; if the user decides to use it, then he or she sends payment to the author of the program. This system is based on trust. And it works: many excellent programs live their lives as shareware and develop into commercial packages. Others are put in the 'public domain' and become freeware, usually with the provision that they not be sold separately or as part of another package. This has kept a constant pressure on commercial vendors of software to keep prices down. One advantage of program development within the public domain/ shareware culture is that the software develops here in closer inter-action with, and input from, users.

More dramatic hacker pressure on the computer corporations came from other developments as well. The appearance of the Apple II in 1977 started the race for the PC market – though it took quite a while for all the actors to realize the potentials here. IBM intro-duced its PC and soon innumerable IBM 'clones' (copies) were popping up everywhere. Competition has been intensive in the rapidly expanding IT marketplace, with 'more and better' being hyped on the consumer. A prerequisite for the volume sale of computer equip-ment has been the development of an 'information ideology'. This ideology, or 'cult', has been criticized by many, notably Theodore Roszak in his book *The Cult of Information*. Increasing amounts of information do not necessarily lead to more knowledge, and much of what is termed the 'computer revolution' is advertising hype with the sole purpose of pushing products on the consumer.

In 1984 another important step related to access was taken. Apple introduced its first Macintosh and the race of the graphic user interface (GUI) was started. What Apple did was to address the issue of ease of use of the technology. Their solution was to leave the text-based command structure of the programmer's world and to offer a system that was much easier to understand and use for 'normal people'. Much of this has become advertisement cliché but the basic idea was to lower the threshold of technical competence needed to start using computer technology. In their GUI choice, Apple raised prices, one of the other parameters of access. Other companies followed suit. The ever more sophisticated graphics, sounds, bleeps and blinking require more powerful computers, and the computer one buys never seems to be complete, given the rapid pace of innovation.

From hacking to communications activism

The 1980s witnessed the further development of the computer revolution from below. This was the closer symbioses of hacker computer knowledge and the commitment of political activism. A new breed of hackers began emerging: the communications activists who started putting 'small scale' computer-mediated communications technology to social use. Their efforts took several directions. One dealt with the content and social uses of the new technology and another with the technology itself.

One development was the growing awareness within progressive communities – especially the peace and environmental movements – that computer-mediated communication could be a powerful tool for their work: gathering and spreading information and enhancing communication between and coordination of individuals and groups locally, nationally and globally. The other, parallel development was the change in the technology itself: computing power was dropping in price and more and more tools for computer-mediated communications were being taken out of their mainframe environments and put into affordable personal computers (PCs). Before there was an Internet running on a universal standard, there were other global networks, some dedicated to putting the new technology to meaningful social use.

Stand-alone BBSes began exchanging data with each other: email, software and 'discussion fora' (sometimes called 'conferences' or 'newsgroups'). When the same data is found in various separate computer-mediated communications systems, we say that it is a mirrored, or distributed system. A widely known system of this type is the USENET, a collection of thousands of newsgroups, open to all. Some types of software, such as the UNIX operating system, are easier to use than others in this kind of system, since communications is built into the operating system, unlike DOS-based systems. Until 80386 processors that allowed for true 32-bit computing were available for PCs, UNIX had to be run in minis or mainframes. As PC hardware became more powerful, and more powerful per dollar, communications software began spreading and developing among the communications activists, who carried the hacker revolution one step further.

One group doing communications development work was found, not unexpectedly, in Menlo Park in the San Francisco Bay Area. From the early 1980s, this group, Community Data Processing (CDP), handled the technical side for the communication activists on the other side of the Bay who were building up PeaceNet and EcoNet, servicing the peace and environmental communities. From this nucleus, several other sister nets appeared, eventually housed together in what is now the Institute for Global Communications (IGC). The IGC and CDP became something of a technical hub for what would later become an international federation, the Association for Progressive Communications. What the 'techies' at CDP managed was to port out a mainframe email and conferencing system to an 80386 PC environment and further develop this into a distributed email and threaded conferencing system. They were first, or among the first, to do this, in an environment that largely held that this could not be done. Each host server, known as a 'node' in such a distributed system, contains the same core of information. This means that an APC user calls to the closest 'node' (APC station) instead of making an international call, or paying for some type of Internet linkage. Before the arrival of a standardized Internet, the nodes connected via high-speed modems. Smaller systems, without leased lines connecting them to the Internet, are still using high-speed modems for their linkages. The tools forged by the communications hackers were brought to social use by the communications activists. The result of this synergy between hackers and activists was that low-cost host servers could be, and were, set up around the globe, directly in the service of individuals and groups working for social change and with issues of planetary survival.

As the Internet and the World Wide Web expanded in the 1990s, new tools were made and new methods of operating introduced. For example, mailing list technology could provide both a tighter control and less information overload than the sometimes cumbersome conferencing (newsgroup) systems.[11] As commercial service provision became less expensive and more widespread, communications activists, especially in the North, began turning to activities other than providing basic access.

The Association for Progressive Communications (APC) is the largest non-commercial NGO network specifically serving the peace and environmental community. The APC operates a distributed email and conferencing/database system as well as electronic publishing and distribution of several news services on a fully global basis. This is run on a non-commercial basis with the specific purpose of strengthening civil society. The goal of the APC is stated in its original charter:

> APC aims to provide a globally interconnected electronic communications network dedicated to a free and balanced flow of information. APC's member organizations serve people working toward goals including peace, the prevention of warfare, elimination of militarism, protection of the environment, furtherance of human rights and the rights of peoples, achievement of social and economic justice, elimination of poverty, promotion of sustainable and equitable development, advancement of participatory democracy, and non-violent conflict resolution.[12]

Organizationally, the APC is a federation of legally and financially independent organizations, each running a 'node' or main station in the global communications system. There is a pooling of technical and organizational resources and a system of cost-sharing.[13] (For history, see info-box.)

In one sense, the APC and like-minded organizations picked up the UNESCO chips after this inter-state organization was pulled off the board as a result of its Third World advocacy of a New World Information and Communication Order. The communication activists started constructing a model for a new global information order with a hands-on, bottom-up approach. One field of activity not covered in this study is the work done by other United Nations agencies such as the UNDP (United Nations Development Program), the UNV (United Nations Volunteers) and the NGLS (United Nations Non-Governmental Liaison Service) in supporting, initiating and facilitating the use of ICT for development, social service and change. The linking of the inter-governmental work of these agencies to NGO networking became visible in the ICT work for the series of UN summits held in the 1990s on various issues of global concern. NGO electronic networking fitted well into the UN strategy of allying with NGOs around the world to lobby for the issues and to be the watchdog over the implementation of inter-governmental agreements.

The 1992 Rio Summit on the environment was something of a breakthrough for global NGO computer networking. This Summit was a revival of UN world summitry intended to focus global attention on areas critical to planetary survival. Other inter-government meetings would follow, and at each there would be a parallel meeting organized by and for NGOs. So a system of global lobbying was built into these meetings, with thousands of participants. This put new demands on informational services, for both broadcasting to the media and communication between participants. This communication was carried on before, during and after the actual conference, the latter as a type of watchdog system so that all the resolutions did not just disappear somewhere in verbal space. Starting with the Rio Summit, the APC has provided electronic information services for the following World Summits called by the United Nations.

As pointed out by Ian Peter, then at Pegasus Networks in Australia, the distribution system provided by the APC networks soon became a major organizer and distributor of UN material for NGOs and governments alike. Because of the speed and ease of electronic communications, the work of these conferences probably became more effective.[14] Shelley Preston, in her article 'The 1992 Rio Summit and Beyond', states that 'these on-site information exchange services were unprecedented at a United Nations conference.'[15] What the Rio Summit meant for the communications activists was that they were no longer being treated as computer nerds on the fringe,

The APC: a brief description

The Association for Progressive Communications (APC) is a global network of networks whose mission is to empower and support organizations, social movements and individuals through the use of information and communication technologies to build strategic communities and initiatives for the purpose of making meaningful contributions to human development, social justice, participatory democracies and sustainable societies.

Initiated in 1990 by 7 founding members, APC is the largest computer network in the world dedicated to NGO networking. One of APC's key operating principles has been to share technical and organizational development knowledge with emerging networks, particularly in the developing world, to build global networking capacity. APC maintains close relations with over 40 partner networks in Africa, Asia and other regions considered not commercially viable by mainstream service providers. Many of APC's partners provide the only NGO computer networking in their country and, therefore, an indispensable link to the global development community. APC's continued support for regional networking development has enabled these networks to undertake collaborations of their own, and to build a local APC presence.

In 1997, APC is a consortium of 25 international member networks, offering vital communication links to over 50,000 NGOs, activists, educators, policy-makers, and community leaders in 133 countries. This dramatic growth reflects a heightened consciousness and use of networking technology by community organizations around the world, as well as a clear recognition that APC has been successful in advocating and facilitating full global access to communications technology and information-sharing, particularly for those in the South.

In providing computer networking services to the local social change community, each APC member network operates independently; however, they offer many services in common and face similar development challenges, though often at a different pace from each other. APC's role has been to coordinate the delivery of common networking and content services across all member networks; to provide a platform for facilitated international APC user communities and projects; and to assist the ongoing operation and development of member networks to meet their evolving needs, as well as those of social change movements around the world.

Source: APC International Secretariat – Brazil * Supporting Electronic Networks; Amalia Souza, Program Coordinator * Email: amalia@apc.org December 1997.

Global Internet Community for Environment, Human Rights, Development & Peace

Home

Members & Services

APC Highlights

Programmes

Communities

About APC

Search

Strategic Uses

Network Development

Content & Tools

Policy Awareness

Women's Programme

APC Africa

Defending the Right to Communicate

New communication technologies are making universal communication possible. Nonetheless, these technologies are concentrated in the same groups that control economic and political power and hegemonize media globally. Co-organised by APC, the International Forum: Communication And Citizenship held in El Salvador September 9-11, 1998, called for the United Nations to convene a World Conference on Communication.

South African Women's Organisations Move Online

Women'sNet is an exciting new networking support programme for women, hosted by APC member, SANGONeT. Launched in March 1998, Women'sNet connects women in South Africa through the Internet to people, information, resources and tools. The Women'sNet site is full of current news, as well as subject-specific information: Preventing Violence against Women, Health, Enterprise and Small Business, Jobs, Human Rights and more. The site was planned and continues to be up-dated by South African women's organisations. To learn more about how it came together, read "Building a Web Site Together - How the Women'sNet Site Was Born".

Mission-Driven Business Planning Project

"Non-profit Internet service provider": Oxymoron? Impossible dream? APC's members are taking part in a unique project to develop innovative business strategies in keeping with APC's mission of supporting social justice and development through strategic use of the Internet.

APC Secretariat

North American Regional Office
Presidio Building 1012
First Floor
Torney Avenue
P.O. Box 29904-0904
San Francisco, CA 94129-0904
USA

tel: +1.415.561.6100 x120
fax: +1.415.561.6101
apcadmin@apc.org

FIGURE 2.1   APC homepage <http://www.apc.org/english.html>

but that non-governmental, non-hierarchical groups could put together and operate an informational distribution and communications system that was more accessible and meaningful than what commercial or government organizations were providing.

The Internet

What is the Internet?

What is known as the Internet is a decentralized, interconnected myriad of computer networks. One history maintains that its decentralized architecture developed out of Cold War military–strategic considerations in the USA to have a computer communications system that would survive a nuclear attack. If part of the system were destroyed, communications could be routed through the remaining parts of the network. The civilian adaptation of the military net became the academically oriented ARPANET in the USA. Most of the early networks were purpose-built, intended for example for a closed community of scholars. The business community had several networks. In the mid-1980s the British JANET and the US NSFNET (National Science Foundation) started a process toward establishing standards so that the various networks could connect to one another. Technically and organizationally this was a rather complicated matter, involving decisions on protocols, gateway and management systems.[16]

The USA took the lead here, with US public spending making the project economically feasible. Since this funding would not continue inevitably, the NSF advocated getting businesses interested in using the information infrastructure that was being built, first at the local and regional levels. Eventually, commercialization of what is now known as the Internet took place.

NSF's privatization policy culminated in April 1995, with the defunding of the NSFNET Backbone. The funds thereby recovered were (competitively) redistributed to regional networks to buy national-scale Internet connectivity from the now numerous, private, long-haul networks

The Backbone had made the transition from a network built from routers out of the research community (the 'Fuzzball' routers from David Mills) to commercial equipment. In its 8½ year lifetime, the Backbone had grown from six nodes with 56 kbps links to 21 nodes with multiple 45 Mbps links. It had seen the Internet grow to over 50,000 networks on all seven continents and outer space, with approximately 29,000 networks in the United States.

Such was the weight of the NSFNET program's ecumenism and funding ($200 million from 1986 to 1995) – and the quality of the protocols themselves – that by 1990 when the ARPANET itself was finally decommissioned, TCP/IP had supplanted or marginalized most other wide-area computer network protocols worldwide, and IP was well on its way to becoming THE bearer service for the Global Information Infrastructure.

The Internet Society's history of the Internet attributes the spread of the Transmission Control Protocol/Internet Protocol (TCP/IP) standard to the openness of the NSF in spreading its documentation. The TCP/IP is an open communications protocol that took shape in the late 1960s and 1970s under the guidance of Bob Kahn. Four ground rules were critical to Kahn's early thinking:

- Each distinct network would have to stand on its own and no internal changes could be required to any such network to connect it to the Internet.
- Communications would be on a best effort basis. If a packet didn't make it to the final destination, it would shortly be retransmitted from the source.
- Black boxes would be used to connect the networks; these would later be called gateways and routers. There would be no information retained by the gateways about the individual flows of packets passing through them, thereby keeping them simple and avoiding complicated adaptation and recovery from various failure modes.
- There would be no global control at the operations level.

While the organizational context for the development of what became Internet standards was somewhat different from that of the hackers, the geography (southern California, MIT) and time frame were the same. So, not surprisingly, the 'Internet ethic' is not unlike what has been called the 'hacker ethic'. There are even more parallels. In 1978, and again in 1988, AT&T/Bell Labs were offered what was then 'the Internet' by US government agencies for free. But they turned the offer down.[17] So the development of what we now know as the Internet was left in the hands of the co-operating community of programmers and communications activists.

Distribution of documentation of TCP/IP was not done by the usual academic methods, but more by what has been called the hacker methodology ('information wants to be free'). This started in 1969 with a system known as the Request for Comments (RFC) series of notes. First distributed by snail mail and then by email, FTP and WWW, these notes became a system of interaction between researchers and hands-on operators, all contributing to a co-operative accumulation of knowledge and development of a shared communications system.

> As the current rapid expansion of the Internet is fueled by the realization of its capability to promote information sharing, we should understand that the network's first role in information sharing was sharing the information about its own design and operation through the RFC documents. This unique method for evolving new capabilities in the network will continue to be critical to future evolution of the Internet.

Over the two decades of Internet activity, there has been a steady evolution of organizational structures designed to support and facilitate an ever-increasing community working collaboratively on Internet issues. A key actor here is the Internet Society.

> The recent development and widespread deployment of the World Wide Web has brought with it a new community, as many of the people working on the WWW have not thought of themselves as primarily network researchers and developers. A new coordination organization was formed, the World Wide Web Consortium (W3C). Initially led from MIT's Laboratory for Computer Science by Tim Berners-Lee (the inventor of the WWW) and Al Vezza, W3C has taken on the responsibility for evolving the various protocols and standards associated with the Web.

The Internet is becoming increasingly commercialized. Originally, commercial efforts mainly comprised vendors providing the basic networking products, and service providers offering the connectivity and basic Internet services. The Internet has now become almost a 'commodity' service, and much present attention has been on the use of this global information infrastructure for support of other commercial services.

The 1990s witnessed the development and rapid adoption of tools for navigating the Internet ('browsers') and for organizing and reading information through a standardized hyper-text mark-up language (HTML). Together, these are commonly known as the World Wide Web technology, which allows users easy access to information linked across the globe. More and more products are available to help organize that information. Many developments in technology are aimed at providing increasingly sophisticated information services on top of the basic Internet data communications. This calls for increasingly sophisticated software and hardware. Some companies are trying to capture the market. The Internet is an evolving system and will continue to change as computing and communications patterns change. This occurs not just because of technical innovations but also according to the uses of the technology.

The politics of the Internet

The Internet is often seen as the basic infrastructure or backbone of that virtual non-place called 'cyberspace'. The commercialization of computing and networking has led to much hype on the graces of high technology. Public discourses have again been carried on about our individual and collective digital futures. The standpoints both reflect basic values and approaches sketched out above and discuss the more specific phenomenon of global networking. The 'politics of the Internet' is increasingly becoming an area not only of academic discourse but of real political conflict. This is around issues of access, governance, ownership and investment, and degrees of autonomy. In keeping with the Gramscian view of the pre-eminence of conflicts over the control of the mode of information, some even predict future 'net wars' and 'cyberocracy'. Perhaps this future is already here, at least judging by some of the literature. David Ronfeldt puts it in the following way in his essay 'Cyberocracy is Coming'.

> What new 'ism' or 'ocracy' may arise? The purpose of this paper is to suggest that 'cyberocracy' is coming. This term, from the roots 'cyber-' and '-cracy', signifies rule by way of information. As it develops, information and its control will become a dominant source of power, as a natural next step in man's political evolution. In the past, under aristocracy, the high-born ruled; under theocracy, the high priests ruled. In modern times, democracy and bureaucracy have enabled new kinds of people to participate in government. In turn, cyberocracy, by arising from the current revolution in information and communications technologies, may slowly but radically affect who rules, how, and why.[18]

Writing from a Fascist prison in the 1920s, Antonio Gramsci analysed the emergence of industrialized culture and the dominating influence of the consciousness-creating information sector. Control over consciousness means hegemony. So while 'cyberocracy' may be a new term, the phenomenon is hardly new. The argument put forward here is that the computer revolution is an attack on an existing cultural and informational hegemony, with victories on a few fronts. This political struggle can be described in several ways. Two Swedish journalists, Lars Ilshammar and Ola Larsmo describe it in their book *net.wars* in the following way.

> For the battle has begun. On the one side are the radical democratic activists with lots of idealism and know-how: on the other side terribly rich corporations. The struggle is about the future public space. The communications revolution that people have talked about for a long time has begun to be filled with a social and political content.[19]

The opposing sides in the struggle have been given many different names, depending upon one's ideological and methodological perspective. But there is a conflict here over both the content and the technology to produce and deliver the content. The computer revolution opened a door for non-hegemonistic individuals and groups to counter the consciousness-creating hegemony of the cultural and informational elites, who are now trying to push that door closed again. But since the computer revolution also created a market for PC peripherals and networked communications and information retrieval, the industry is also working against itself. Broadened access means more money, but also the possibility of losing control and sprouting innumerable alternatives to hegemonistic media. The caveat here is that business is only interested in those people who can pay, thereby excluding the potentially more dangerous global majority who cannot pay for the equipment and services. Since the market maintains an impetus toward ever more sophisticated machinery, it helps maintain the class-differentiating nature of computing, with some exceptions. One exception is those companies who realize that there is a profitable low end of the market, especially when added on to other services such as telephones and digital television. Another exception would be those groups, organizations and movements who consciously adapt and develop technologies to widen access, especially for people in the South. Since access is such an important aspect of using ICT, it will be treated in a little more detail.

Barriers to access

There are several types of barriers to access to the benefits of computer-mediated communications. These aspects will now be dealt with, one by one.

Money Not everyone can afford a 'modern' computer, whatever that may be. By constantly 'upgrading' software that needs ever more powerful machines to operate on, many people are simply denied access to what is defined as necessary to take part in the information revolution. Now, much of this is hype. The widest personal use of CMC, electronic mail, can be run off the simplest PC; no graphics required. In fact, even text-based uses of the WWW can be accessed with a very simple machine. Another cost is for connectivity: for most people in the world access to a personal telephone is still a luxury far beyond the horizon. Access to electricity can be a major barrier.

There is a political economy of the bandwidth, for the simple reason that cables and connections that can operate at high and super-high speeds cost money. Simple email and other text-based communications can be done at 'slow speeds'. But video-on-demand or game-playing over the Internet requires lots of speed (bandwidth). So the list of different types of ICT technologies presented on page 51 is also a graph of its own political economy.

Ease of use A major barrier to using CMC (and computers) is ease of use. Running the machine (any machine) can be difficult, especially one that only does exactly what you tell it to and has zero per cent error margins. The early computers were designed for, and by, computer specialists who never imagined that the computer would become a household appliance. When computer manufacturers decided that there was a consumer market for these machines, they then began looking for ways to increase 'user friendliness'. This easiness of use had to be weighed against cost since – as things were to develop – greater user friendliness usually means higher cost (which this author finds very unfriendly – like having a friend invite you out for dinner and then letting you pick up the bill).

Language The *lingua franca* of computers is English. For many, using a computer is a test of their knowledge of this language of globalism.

Types of information and communications technology

Email Electronic mail is basically one-to-one communication, with a digitalized piece of information sent from one user to another user's mailbox on any host that maintains a valid mailbox for that user. Copies can be sent to other users' mailboxes. Email technology has been expanded so that many-to-many communication is possible through the use of *mailing lists*. Email can be done either online or offline.

Conferencing Electronic conferences are thematically indexed folders of communications. The user of a conference can read, reply to topics or write a new topic, depending on the type of conference. Some are read-only, some are open to all for both reading and writing, and some are closed, open only to accepted members. Some conferences are moderated, with the moderator letting users in and sometimes editing the material. Conferencing can be done either online or offline. Newsgroup is another name for an electronic conference.

FTP The File Transfer Protocol is a tool for moving files from a server to your service provider's machine, and then moving them (downloading) to a user's machine. Retrieving files through FTP can be done either online or offline.

Gopher This is a tool that creates menus that allows a user to access network resources by moving an on-screen pointer. A gopher can point to text files, telnet sites for linking to another remote computer, and other types of data. Basically online.

World Wide Web A program that works through hypertext links to data, allowing a user to explore network resources from multiple entry points. WWW has for many become synonymous with the hypertext servers connected to one another via the Internet. Basically online. The WWW can be either text-based or, in its most popular form, use a graphical interface. The WWW is moving rapidly toward webcasting with audio and video.

In this author's opinion, the development and spread of operating systems, manuals, programs and instructional materials in languages other than English has not proceeded very fast. With linguistic dominance comes cultural dominance. Many in the South are beginning to fear that the spread of ICT might mean McCulture strengthening its hegemonic grip.

Connectivity CMC rests upon being connected to a server that in turn is connected to other host servers. Until now, the usual way to do this for ordinary people is through the telephone line. Nonordinary people, like college professors, can sit in front of their computer, or computer terminal, connected through a physical, direct wire to a server, in turn connected through cabling to other host servers. So, at a minimum, a user has to have access to a phone line that can be used for dialling a server, or go to a place where a terminal connection is available. Obviously, the easier the connectivity, the wider the use.

Information overload Information overload is a widely experienced phenomenon. This is not only due to computers, but is a fact of modern or post-modern life. Having too much to choose from can sometimes be inhibiting and may pose a barrier for some people. But there is another aspect to information load that is more specific to computer-mediated communication and the informational relationship between North and South. That the North has a technological advantage is obvious, an advantage that may be increasing and one that may turn out to be a keystone in maintaining all the other advantages that the North has over the South. So there is some scepticism among would-be users of the new communications technologies that this may open the door to yet another wave of informational dominance from the North (see page 55 for two examples).

Irrelevancy Going out on the Net means becoming exposed to information that may be experienced as irrelevant, or worse. Electronic junk mail gets dropped unrequested into my emailbox, just as junk paper mail gets dropped into my paper mailbox. This spamming is a real problem for many, if for no other reason than that it clouds some of the more positive uses of email in mists of irrelevancy.

Reliability   Since email and Internet services are both new and no-where near universal, a real concern is whether or not my email really gets there, and gets picked up and read. Do the servers really connect to one another? Did I use the correct address? This is in addition to concerns over my own software and hardware problems.

Availability of know-how   It requires training to use the new technol-ogy, even if one of the lasting contributions of the computer revo-lution in the form of the dispersion of personal computing has been to lower the knowledge threshold. While computers tend to become easier to use, an input of education is required. A lack of this is a serious barrier.

Computer culture   There are several aspects of the internal computer culture that tend to act as barriers to access. One is the development of a special lingo called computerese. Mastery of this language de-fines who is in and who is excluded. The computer culture has been predominantly 'pale and male': another way of preserving and ex-tending white male supremacy. More of this later. The computer culture has been marketed in a yuppie package. What has been called the 'politics of the interface' reflects this.

Even the interface on the personal computer has its own politics. The politics of the GUI – Graphic User Interface – be it Macintosh or Windows, is clearly that of corporate culture. Both the terminol-ogy and the desktop iconography reflect this. There are clocks and calendars, filing cabinets and spreadsheets, telephones and clipboards. The message is clear: we are to order our lives in a business-like fashion. Why a business desktop? Why not a kitchen? Or a play-ground? A garden? Or a woodworking shop? A village?

Fear of misuse   One barrier to access is also the fear that the new technology is, or might be, used for criminal or retrograde purposes. Several pieces of legislation have been propelled by these fears of criminality, of pornography, trafficking in child abuse, of hate mail being pushed on people, racist propaganda, and so on. These fears and the phenomena that arouse them are real and have to be taken into account when discussing the spread of ICT. One such fear is that the spread of ICT might mean the end of privacy. Not one 'Big

Brother' watching us all, but lots of little brothers spying on and bothering each other.

The politics of the link   Information overload and putting 'the world's biggest library', the WWW, in the middle of a seemingly endless shopping mall confuses many people. Another barrier to access is not being informed about what is available. During my work on this book's chapter on Bosnia, I tapped nearly all available sources of information on the WWW. I became aware of how linking was politicized. 'Linking' is the phenomenon of providing access for one's own website (home page) to another, or other 'pages' or websites. When provided and used well, this is the heart of 'surfing the Internet': one source leads to another, to a third and so on. The intelligent and service-minded webmaster can lead his readers to other information, as well as himself avoid duplication of effort. So linking can be used to establish virtual communities of interest. But linking can also be used politically, as the examples described on the next page show.

During the intensive period of NATO intervention in the war in Bosnia, I analysed not only the grassroots networking taking place, but also government uses of CMC and Internet broadcasting as well as the commercial media. The Cable News Network, CNN, a major actor in the war in Bosnia, was already using the WWW to re-broadcast its material, as well as providing complementary material that could not be provided on television. As a part of its WWW service, CNN also provided 'links' to other sources of information on the WWW. What were these links? The CNN provided links to WWW sites maintained by the Serbian government but not to the grassroots peace movements. This pattern was not unique to CNN, but was also followed by other media corporations. This choice of links is even more puzzling when we consider that the media, especially CNN, were pointing to the Serb government of rump-Yugoslavia as a main perpetrator in the conflict. This pattern may be general: that the media corporations do not 'down-link', meaning censoring of sources that could provide alternatives, media substitution. On the other hand, the grassroots networks, like the ZaMir Transnational Net in the Bosnian conflict, provided ample 'up-links' to the media corporations.

Access disparity and info-dumping: two examples

In a conversation with a colleague at St Joseph's College in Turichua-palli in southern India, the topic of the information gap arose. Not surprising, since the professor in question lectures to my students about the causes and effects of globalization. One problem he faces, especially apparent when his students are doing graduate research, is the availability of material, even on India. Comparing notes, we easily surmised that it was easier for me and my students, sitting at our computers in Sweden, to obtain material on India than it is for him and his students, sitting in India, in the midst of what they are studying; and that this information gap is probably growing due to the way in which the world is wiring up. The spread of the Internet and WWW is a top-down process, since it involves initially con-siderable sums of money and access to other resources. So in India, it is the information brokers who are first out and it is not surprising to find many Indian daily newspapers as well as magazines available on the Internet. Sitting in Stockholm, I have direct, immediate access to *The Hindu*, published in Chennai, along with other economic publications, while my professor friend, further down in the same state, does not. This was in 1997.

Another example is a story told to me by a participant in a computer training seminar I taught at in New Delhi. This was for NGOs doing social and development work. Many of these organi-zations have contacts with support groups in the North. One gentle-man told me about his first nightmarish experience with electronic mail. As soon as their support group in the USA found out that they had installed email in their office in India, they started sending large amounts of information via email to their Indian friends. And the Indian organization discovered that a whole month's salary was spent merely on the connection costs for picking up this information dump. Although well-meant and sent with good intentions, it was still an information dump and a drain on local resources.

Electronic colonialization   A very real fear in the South is that of cultural penetration from the North by means of the new information and communication technologies. This is both in terms of form and content. ICT is seen by many as a new tool for spreading 'world culture', a euphemism for 'McCulture' in the popular sphere and the paradigm of Western science as the definition of knowledge, subduing culture-specific forms of knowledge.[21]

Using intellectual property rights clauses in international trade agreements, the North can maintain domination of the software needed to operate the technology. The concentration of information resources and online publics in the North means that much of the digital information circulating the globe originates in the North. Even within social movements there has been a wariness towards distributed conferencing since this can be experienced as expensive, as info-dumping, and as a way for the North to impose Northern definitions of relevancy. One result is that it is email that has so far been the major demand from movements in the South. The mailing list tool, described on page 57, seems to be growing in popularity in the South, since it decentralizes a selective control of information and of who may participate. Concretely, Northerners can be excluded from Southern discourses.[22]

Barrier jumping

Barriers are there, according to the hacker ethic, to be jumped. Realizing that most people in this world do not have access to computers, phones, modems and Internet accounts, several technological tools have been developed to at least provide access to high-end information with very low-end, bare-bones technology (see page 51). These types present us with a simple political economy of CMC. Access depends directly on the amount of money you have – and where you are living. Technologies have been developed that build around the fact that it is email that is the type of CMC most readily accessible and this in an offline mode to keep connect time to a minimum to save money. For email, nearly any computer suffices and nearly any modem. A litmus test of the political economy of a network, or CMC system, would be how seriously it takes this supposition. Just a few examples of the possibilities are presented here.

The one-to-one communication of email can be expanded through *mailing lists*. These are topical lists to which one subscribes. Some are 'read-only' while others are 'interactive', meaning that a subscriber can contribute by sending an email to the list, which then gets added on to. In this way, a discussion and information exchange can be carried on. While some lists are maintained manually, there are several different software packages running on computer hosts that can automate this. Thus email can become both one-to-many and many-to-many. Otherwise, it is the *conference* that was developed first as the tool for many-to-many communication. But since not all servers do conferencing and not all users can afford online participation in conferences, cost-cutting tools have been developed. Some hosts repost conferences as mailing lists. Since this can entail large volumes of information, this can be done in two steps. First, a user can request an index. After receiving and examining the index, the user can then request specific items in the list (conference). In this way, a user can avoid becoming an 'information dump' as described above. This is then a way of trying to avoid superfluous messages in electronic discussion fora. There are also software packages that allow for offline conferencing. Offline readers can thus be for both email and conferencing.

Larger chunks of information are sometimes put into what is known as an *FTP archive*. Using what is known as anonymous FTP-mail, files can be requested by email from the archive. For those who can afford longer connection times to a host computer, either leased line or modem, and have the necessary machines, there is the high end of surfing the WWW at websites and gopher archives, and so on.

Computer Lib: Round II

One challenge to commercialized information technology, with a strong inherent trend toward monopolistic control, is coming from the GNU project and the Free Software Foundation. The basic idea here is very simple and straightforward: computer software is a set of tools and should be made available to everyone. No one should own these tools, since ownership can mean denial of access, either through pricing and/or regulation (depending upon who claims ownership). The legal technique used to keep free software free is anti-copyright copyrighting. 'Free' here does not relate to price but to control. This is the GNU General Public License (GPL). Under the GPL, authors 'copyleft' their programs so that no one can take out patents on them or further applications or versions of their components. This reverse use of intellectual property rights may seem complicated at first but is a clarification of some basic issues of information technology. *If* this technology is, as many claim, reshaping the world *and* the way we perceive the world, *then* it is extremely important, from a democratic viewpoint, that the basic tools of this reshaping and perceiving are accessible to all. I have already made this point in an analogy: as an author I can copyright this book but neither I nor anyone else can copyright the English language.

One important project following the copyleft path is Linux. This is a near-UNIX operative system first developed by the Finnish programmer Linus Torvalds. Many others have added to its development, in terms of the kernel, system and application. And this is the whole point: the creation of a community of programmers developing operative systems and applications with each other. This is done through openness, sharing and crazy experimentation. This is a repetition of what Stephen Levy described so well in his book *Hackers – Heroes of the Computer Revolution*. But instead of a small group sitting in an MIT lab, the new community is global. Yet the culture and ethic persist.

I have noticed an interesting phenomenon since the arrival of Linux around 1991. Nearly every programmer, systems administrator and, to a lesser extent, salesperson I have met knows about Linux and usually has a copy running on his/her own PC. And, scratching the surface, I discover that most have a fairly good sense of why they do this: as a gesture of independence in the face of an increasingly monopolistic world of computing that is closing in on itself. Open systems are challenges to the imagination. They can be changed, made to do new things, *played with* in a field of autonomous action.

Other software applications of importance have been, and are being, developed in the spirit of the GPL/copyleft arrangement. Examples are the widely spread email program Eudora from the University of Illinois in Urbana, the PINE ('Program for Internet News and Email') package of software from the University of Washington for DOS, Windows and UNIX platforms, Minuet from the University of Minnesota, and the Arachne project from a group in Czechia. Arachne is an attempt to produce a full-fledged WWW package for both clients and servers.

A challenge to Microsoft's monopoly on operating systems for PCs is coming from the Linux Community. The Linux Community is a community with a cause, some critics say 'a religion'.[23] There are many projects, coordinating bodies, a grant fund, a journal, online publications and a global network all providing the 'glue' for the community. GLUE also stands for 'Groups of Linux Users Everywhere'.[24] The cause is explicit: to keep software 'free' ('in the sense of free speech, not free beer'). And the concrete meaning of this is to provide an operative system platform that challenges Microsoft or any other corporation that tries to close things in. This challenge is through price and flexibility. Since there are no copyright or patent fees on the kernel, and there is an abundance of freeware, this is especially attractive to the South and educational institutions. The flexible openness of Linux appeals to many businesses and challenges the intelligence and creativity of many users and programmers, who are invited to make it better.[25]

In a sense, GPL provided a written constitution for the new online tribe of Linux hackers. The license said it was OK to build on, or incorporate wholesale, other people's code – just as Linux did – and even to make money doing so (hackers have to eat, after all). But you couldn't transgress the hacker's fundamental law of software: source code must be freely available for further hacking.

In March 1994, the official Linux 1.0 appeared, almost as a formal declaration of independence. By then the user base was already large, and the core Linux development team substantial. Among the thousands of files Linux contains, there is one called simply Credits. In it are the names, addresses, and contributions of the main Linux hackers. The list runs to more than 100 names, scattered around the world. Almost uniquely for a hacker project, Linux has huge and comprehensive sets of FAQs, how tos, and general help files (see, for example, the Linux Documentation Project)....

Staying on top may prove increasingly difficult for Microsoft. The latest version of Linux – release 2.0 – offers 64-bit processing (NT and many Unixes are only 32-bit); symmetric multiprocessing, which allows the simultaneous deployment of several chips in a system; and networking more advanced than that of any other operating system.

A related advantage of Linux's developmental structure is that security fixes typically turn up faster than from commercial suppliers. For example, when a 'Ping of Death' assault of multiple, low-level messages crashed several operating systems worldwide, a quick patch to Linux enabled the attack to be thwarted in a couple of hours. 'Somebody posted a report of the ping,' recalls Alan Cox, author of the fix, 'so I just sat down, fixed it, and posted the fix straight back.' Users of other operating systems had to sweat out their vulnerability far longer.

... Yet Linux's importance lies not just in the size of its installed base, but also where those users are found. 'More than 120 countries are represented according to Alvestrand. 'And Linux is a real power in the less developed countries – in some cases growing faster than the Internet.'[26]

Besides the academic community, businesses started to pick up on Linux, one source even stating the opinion that probably more development work had gone into the latest Linux kernel than went in to Windows NT. And Linux is moving beyond 'catching up' into true development. A free operating system has appeared, produced by a community of advocates, in the second round of computer liberation.

As the boundaries between an operating system (OS) and the Internet become more and more blurred, systems such as Linux may come and go. But what is increasingly being known as the 'Open Source Movement' is growing. And it is not confined to academic ivory-tower programmers, reclusive hackers or computer radicals. While including these elements, the movement is being institutionalized and is gaining ground in the business community. More and more professional software producers are putting their packages on the Linux platform. In 1998, Netscape (re)joined the movement and released its source code, inviting the broader community of programmers to join in on developmental work. SUN (Stanford University Networks) has joined Linux International. As pointed out by the *Linux Journal*, it is not only possible for software developers to make money working on an open source philosophy; it may even be counterproductive for the economy as a whole to continue the system of intellectual property rights for most software.[27] This question and the debate around it may prove to be of central importance, and will be returned to in the concluding chapter.

Types of Alternative Network

A network is a system for receiving and transmitting information. A network can be based on computers, computer terminals, other types of electronic equipment, including just plain telephone lines. The terms 'network' and 'networking' have both technical and sociological meanings. Sometimes the meanings overlap – as they do here in a definition provided by John Quarterman in his book *The Matrix:*

> Network users group together in a variety of ways related to the under-lying technology or to mutual interest. The networks and conferencing systems themselves produce communities of convenience of people with access to the same services and interfaces. More specialized communities form from interest and accessibility, whether on a single system or across several.
> ... Networks may be not only communities of convenience, but also communities of interest. Many of them form around people who are involved in the same sorts of activities. Here are some examples of com-munities of researchers, of communities formed around certain kinds of facilities or around the use of certain software, and of political commu-nities.[28]

There are networks for scientific research and for business-computer centres. Some are built around operating systems, both large and small. Computer networking is used by political communities. Quarterman points out that there is a tendency to connect small, independent facilities to one another.[29] The reasons for this are several: the general impetus to a broader access, perhaps an inherent dynamic. For many network makers, the medium is the message – that is, communicative action is in itself a political act. In the words of Graham Lane, 'networking becomes a way of life'. The application of information technology as computer-mediated communication may be network-creating, in that it in itself links groups and individuals otherwise isolated from each other, as well as facilitating communica-tion and information distribution within already established networks.

Communitarians

Although the original Community Memory project at Berkeley – the terminal at Leopold's Records – was closed down, the type of thinking and practice it represented took root. The thinking here was to use the new technology to salvage and reconstruct a disintegrating social vortex through computer networking. More and more studies were showing that local communities, defined as social networks, were falling apart, families were becoming isolated and individuals were, to use Robert Putnam's phrase, 'bowling alone'. In his book *The Spirit of Community* Amitai Etzioni argues that the defence and reconstruction of democracy needs to be based on a revitalization of civil society, based on communitarian values.[30] While philosophers and academic analysts were studying the need for the reconstruction of civil society, others, following the 'hands-on' approach, were doing something about it.

One communitarian use of computer-mediated communication is the WELL (Whole Earth 'Lectronic Link). This system developed out of a desire to provide a means for people to exchange information and ideas, to communicate. Through his books *Virtual Reality* and *The Virtual Community,* Howard Rheingold has made this Bay Area bulletin board system one of the most widely publicized experiments in community computing. (In computerese, 'virtual' means 'in the computer' or 'on the Net' as opposed to 'outside the computer' – that is, the real world and real-life communities.[31]) While the WELL has never seemed to have shed its 'yuppie' (or post-pothead) image, many other experiments in community computing have emerged. The goal is not to have people disappear into virtual worlds of the computer and networks ('surfing alone') but to make people known and visible to each other in the real world; in other words, to strengthen 'natural' or local communities.

In North America, entire networks of community networks and FreeNets have emerged. Academic interest in these networks has been aroused. There are several evaluations of these types of networks, their structures, and even the economic impact on their communities. Since these community networks are electronic networks, a good deal of (self-)interest in them is reflected on the Net – that is, the World Wide Web. So a natural starting place for resources is the WWW Virtual Library, which maintained a starting guide to these community networks, as well as writings on and around them.[32] Kim Gregson at the School of Library and Information Science, Indiana University, has compiled a bibliography and resource guide on community networks.[33] In her study *Communities On-Line*, Anne Beamish found that community networks were finding it difficult to reconstruct civil society.

Most community networks are rich in local information, ranging from job opportunities to minutes of the city council meetings. But, surprisingly, in spite of the intention to increase a sense of community and democratic participation, many community networks provide limited opportunity for public debate and discussion. In addition, most community networks do not provide electronic access to elected officials or municipal government staff.[34]

In Britain, the Manchester Host is an example of a government-funded attempt to explore the possibilities of strengthening a local community in transition through community computing. This has been replicated elsewhere in a whole system of 'FreeNets'.

Radical democrats

'Electronic democracy', like communitarian computing, has also become an area of both political and academic interest. This other use of computer-mediated communication is what radical democrats see as something of an electronic town-meeting. Besides pursuing a public discourse of issues and opinions, the technology could make it possible to conduct online voting. While this approach may help to re-enfranchise the electorate, it still has problems in dealing with the selectorate – those who set the agenda and choose those who set the agenda and pose the questions. However, the possible uses for strengthening direct democracy are still young and experimental.

Another, not so radical, use of CMC is for increasing the information flow between elected and electorate. One can now email many heads of government and other political decision-makers, and get an automated response thanking one for viewpoints offered or questions asked. Opening the conduits of information technology has shown for many a politician that this is yet another way of lobbying for interests and favours and perhaps not the hoped for electronic agora for considered public discourse.

Another brand of radical democrats are the 'e-activists'. The approach here is that electronic communication, information broadcasting and retrieval *in itself* has the power to transform. New forms and areas of communication and information exchange are made possible by the new information technologies. These high-tech forms and areas are seen as the new arenas for action. Politics becomes 'cyberpunk' and freedom of thought and expression is taken seriously, in a vein reminiscent of the Berkeley Free Speech Movement of the 1960s. A 1997 example of this electronic activist culture can be found at Steve Mizrach's *Activism Subpage*.[35]

The world of cyber-whatever is severely framed by real politics in a very real world. Here are just a few of the framing factors: electricity

– who gets it, at what price and at what quality; phones, or other types of connectivity – who gets it at what price and at what quality; computers – who gets them; the software necessary to run the computer – who owns it and who controls its development and which applications can be used on the operating system. All these factors are determined politically, not only in the sense of rich people/ poor people but also in terms of laws and regulations concerning pricing in monopolies, patents and intellectual property rights. This emerging communications and information regime is drawing up an arena for politics in the information age.

Perhaps in a realization of a growing distance between e-activism and real-world social movements, an organization called «NetAction» was founded in 1996 'in order to promote effective grassroots citizen action campaigns by creating coalitions that link online activists with grassroots organizations' As a part of this, a collection process was started of 'information about the early uses of the Internet for political advocacy and organizing.'[36] The Political Participation Project at the MIT AI lab has resulted in some studies, for example Mark S. Bonchek's study on how increasing use of CMC may facilitate political participation.[37] Many studies are still at the survey stage, often within the confines of statist definitions of democracy.[38]

Libertarians have been quick to pick up on the possibilities of technology for protecting and enhancing free speech and open news flows. So it is not surprising that many interesting experiments in the use of Internet-based audio and video – that is, radio and television – have a libertarian flavour. RealNetworks (formerly Progressive Networks) seems to be carrying the technological banner with their development and the wide distribution of their software packages (RealPlayer) and support to their project WebActive. Numerous actors are arriving at the Internet from a history in public – that is, listener-supported traditional – radio, for example Pacifica Radio (see Webography). The new forms of 'webcasting' are opening up new channels for 'the other news' and for a highly decentralized system of production and distribution of radio and television. The supersite One World Online has started a radio news service, providing redistribution of radio programmes and a network of radio stations and organizations producing audio materials for Internet distribution.

Communications activists

The emerging grassroots networks are examples of the conscious development of a communicative praxis that uses while questioning the ideological and power base of existing information technology. These 'people-to-people' or NGO networks are outside the industrial–business–governmental sphere. They link intentional communities. These are real-world communities of purpose, people joined together in common causes. Some co-operate with inter-state agencies, public information monopolies, the academic networks and the amateur 'hacker' networks. These new NGO networks offer something innovative and dynamic. Quarterman, stressing the sociological aspects of networking, suggests that these may be the 'true' networks, since they are non-commercial, with human communication as their primary, often only, goal.[39]

Unlike the communitarian and radical democratic uses of CMC, the communication activist approach has not received much attention outside its own sphere. Little systematic academic 'knowledge' has been produced in the sense of this area being announced as a new field of research, with bibliographies being compiled and grants pouring in.

There are exceptions, of course, but it may be that these exceptional treatments of the uses of CMC for social change may contain some answers to this state of affairs: that this tool may be empowering to the point of being dangerous to the planetary status quo. It will be argued that the social movements that use the technology subordinate this use to social and political purposes and do not believe that there is a technological 'fix' to social and economic problems. So scholars looking for 'computerization movements' would be disappointed by communications activists. In other words, the communitarians and radical democrats provide much more independent importance to the technology than the social activists do. Another reason may be that it is hard to be 'objective' in the sense of traditional positivist science. As John Dewey put it long ago, there are two types of knowledge: that of the spectator and that of the actor or participant. It seems that studying how CMC is being used for social and political change appeals mostly to the latter category. Most of the studies on this, including the present one, have been done by people who are or have been actively engaged in what they are writing about. There is a very good qualification to the above, namely in the work done by Internet pioneer John December in his online *CMC Magazine* (1994–99), which covers many areas of social uses of computer-mediated communication and his resource link. But then, he, too, is a 'participant'.

The next two chapters present examples of how CMC has been used by social movements and voluntary associations. Before turning to these examples, here is a brief review of some more widely known effects of CMC.

Some Basic Effects of Computer-Mediated Communication

The creation of differentiation is part of post-modern life.[40] ICT creates differentiation and, with it, the proliferation of subcultures. Some go even farther, claiming the collapse of geography in a 'global de-localization', or 'glocality'. One of these subcultures is the email community, with a strong and expanding foothold in the academic community. Here, there is a subculture within the subculture of academia with a differentiation between those who have it (email) and can use it and those who don't or can't. The difference is between those travelling in a mythical cyberspace and those still in the pedestrian stone age of snail mail and paper memos.

'Email' has emerged as a whole new genre of writing, and is being treated as such by large groups of teachers and scholars.[41] Electronic communication has a strong drawing power. And, as a number of studies would suggest, one-to-one email is probably the single largest use – depending, of course, upon how one defines 'use'. Put in another way: from the user perspective, most people use CMC for electronic mail to some other person. The reasons are obvious: electronic mail saves time and, calculating marginally, even money. This is especially true in the rural South (see pages 68–9).

Many a high-school teacher and college instructor can testify to the enormous drawing power of the online, multi-user programs such as the MUDDs ('Multi-User Dungeons and Dragons') that distract from course-work. Some learning institutions have even banned these from their systems since students would rather communicate than do their homework. Part of the growing folklore of the Net are the various uses of the 'chat' areas, where users can log in and communicate with one another in real time. One such use of chatting is that of digital lonely hearts clubbing, with people finding friends and mates. This is another example of the drawing power of the technology for communication.

When presenting the possibilities of CMC to new groups and demonstrating a specific system (in my case, APC) for new groups, one request always arises. This is to look through the user database to find out if there is someone on the system who is known to someone in the audience. This usually starts off with real persons, and expands into shared membership in an organization or common interest area, sometimes a specific geographical area. Since CMC use is spreading rapidly, some point of connection is usually found. I once had a young second-generation Estonian refugee in Sweden find that his uncle in Tallinn was using the system, and quickly sent a message to him. (This was when the KGB was still opening papermail.) A group of students and teachers in a Swedish folk high school (community college) found, during one such demonstration, that people they knew and knew of in Brazil were connected to the system. Greetings were sent and everyone was impressed.

De-medialization

Why do people get impressed by this? The postal system, in spite of everything, is still the most universal system for communicating. Everybody has a letterbox and pen and paper is more accessible than a computer, modem and telephone. One answer is, of course, technological novelty. There is still some magic in electronic letters and screens, the blips and burps of the future. But there is something more. There is a stronger presence; the persons I am communicating with are, in some way, present in my act of communicating. This is perhaps due to the speed of communication (and the fact that most people don't really understand how it works). The aspect of *performance* is stronger: by sending an email message I am not just communicating a portion of information; I am also establishing an invisible electronic linkage that can be used later. It becomes a symbolic act. I have become part of an interaction, perhaps a network.

Internetting from Vellakulam…

Vellakulam is a very small village on the Marakkanam Road, about half way between Tindivanam and Marakkanam on the Coromandel Coast of Tamil Nadu in south India. An Indian social action group, the Village Community Development Society (VCDS) has a training centre here. In the field since 1980, the VCDS is working with and for the local community of Dalits (outcastes or untouchables) and women, providing non-formal education for working children, quarry workers, handicapped children, and more recently redeveloping non-chemical farming. The VCDS services about sixty villages. The training programmes are geared toward social change by developing a local, rural grassroots leadership that can guide the process of democratization. An important part of this work is linking up to other SAGs (social action groups) around the district, the State of Tamil Nadu, India and the world. Sending a letter through the postal system costs one rupee for national mail and eleven rupees for an international letter. So electronic communication makes economic sense, especially for international communication.

Sending a fax from the booth in Tindivanam, 14 kilometres away, costs about Rs. 100 per page, Rs. 20 to receive a fax. The daily wage for a female agricultural worker is about Rs. 30, a kilo of rice costs a minimum of Rs. 16. Now that the telephone is connected to the centre office, local and trunk calls can be made, but not international calls. Even using a fax machine at the home of someone in town, an international fax would still cost nearly Rs.100 per page.

With a hundred-dollar used laptop and a twenty-five-dollar modem, I can make a trunk call to Chennai (Madras) to EasyLink BBS, connected to the Internet. <www.xlweb.com> Since the lines are usually clogged, I set my communications program to auto and it keeps on churning until the call is placed, the email sent and picked up. The on-line time for several letters runs to about one to one-and-a-half minutes. The cost for a one minute call is Rs. 6. Now $125 may not seem like much, but it represents two months' wages in Vellakulam, or schooling for four handicapped children for a year. However, since a computer can also be used for word-processing

VCDS Centre in Vellakulam, South India – now part of our 'global village' (*J.Walch*)

and accounting, it replaces typewriters, calculators and ledgers, the marginal cost for CMC is more reasonable, when one counts in the savings on postage and faxes.

What can be done with CMC from this corner of the periphery? Walking through the gate, down the Marakkanam Road to the left, the basis for a report on the embezzlement of European Union funds for the desiltation of the village tank can be found. Or cycling the other way to the stone quarry, we can witness the World Bank funding of child labour – children breaking stones for the new national highway. Or further afield pogroms against Dalits.

The case study presented below is that of how communication activists organized the use of ICT in a war zone, during the war over Bosnia in the 1990s. On 25 May 1995 a marketplace was shelled, scores of men, women and children were killed and hundreds wounded (see Chapter 3 for an eyewitness account). The scene of the crime and close-ups of the victims were displayed on television in living rooms around the globe. What was the reaction to this 'genocide live'? What does 'knowing about genocide' mean? Analysts would, and probably will in future studies, agree that the media were actors in this conflict, and try to find ways of measuring when and how much the medialization of this war influenced the military intervention by the international community.

One fact of this intervention is obvious: that it took too long to materialize. Why? There are surely many reasons and explanations for this. But we need also to look into the contradiction of media such as television, a medium that regulates the viewer to a spectator, not a participant. Fortunately, some people refuse this role and can immediately start a support action when they see someone on the television suffering in some far away place. For most of us, medialization is comforting, a confirmation that we are not there. This is not moralizing: since the medium is one-way, I simply cannot respond. Computer-mediated communication provides us with a different possibility. During an academic demonstration of the use of ICT in the Bosnian war I took up an online conference dealing with refugees in ex-Yugoslavia. The index looks like this:

exyugo.refugee – exyugo.refugees

5/20/95	169*serbian police: another repression *ZENSKI_CENTAR@ZAMIR-BG.co*
5/30/95	170*Women in Black Belgrade on refugee *gn:peacenews* 171*SPE/PISMA Mail Update May 30 *pnbalkans*
6/08/95	172*Human Rights Television/Bosnia *dschechter*
6/14/95	173*peace project-volunteers *engel@fub46.zedat.fu-berl* 174*Counseling for Refugees? *espresso1am*
6/16/95	175*Seeking Muhamed Imamovic *grrchicago* 176*SPE Requests Australian help *pnbalkans*
6/23/95	177*weeklu roundup *BETA_BG@ZAMIR-BG.comlink.*
6/29/95	178*SPE/PISMA Update June 28 *pnbalkans*
7/06/95	179*job opportunity in Croatia women's *CENZENA_ZG@ZAMIR-ZG.comli*
7/14/95	180*GESELLSCHAFT FUeR BEDROHTE VOeLKER

GFBV-GERMANY@OLN.comlink.

7/20/95	181*1993: Abandonment of Bosnia *rbleier*
7/28/95	182*Predlog Zakona o drzavljanstvu *SRJ*
	H.ODBOR_BG@ZAMIR-BG.ztn.a
8/08/95	183*Appeal from Bosnian Foreign Ministe *gn:support*
8/12/95	184*Magazine wants to hear from students *pnbalkans*
8/18/95	185*This is Tuzla *1 M.ADO@ZAMIR-TZ.comlink.ap*
8/31/95	186*–> Sarajevo Winter Appeal *pnbalkans*
9/10/95	187*BETA News Agency – Hels. odbor
	BETA_BG@ZAMIR-BG.comlink.

Continuing my improvised demonstration, I took up topic number 185. This is what appeared (spelling corrected):

Conf? 185
M.ADO   exyugo.refugees   7:02 PM Aug 18, 1995
(at ZAMIR-TZ.comlink.apc.org)   (From News system)

Is there anybody out there can you hear my song.
This is Tuzla, so write before I get killed.

For me, a response was imperative.

Conf? 185.1
Topic 185   This is Tuzla   Response 1 of 1
nn:jim   exyugo.refugees   10:57 PM Oct 19, 1995

Yes, we hear you loud and strong, even in the cornfields of Indiana, USA. Good luck...
Jim Walch and friends

At least one college teacher to whom I showed this sequence said she changed her idea about what computers should be used for. Others I have showed this to have concurred. So I started using this example in my teaching and found that generally my listeners are given something real and serious to think about. What can this be? In this type of communication, reality is not filtered. It becomes 'de-mediated'. I am a participant, not a spectator. Receiving reality in de-mediated mode can be very frightening. I have to think for myself. This aspect of ICT may prove to be of long-term importance since it may be a way to break the conceptual hegemony that mediated knowledge and information implies. But the lack of autonomous knowledge structures in which to incorporate the mass of new information is problematic. It is a major intellectual challenge to construct such autonomous conceptual structures.

Other effects

Networks seem to have effects on their users beyond their immediate practical uses. Human interaction increases. This can lead to increased productivity through increased and better use of ideas and documentation. Even informal communications tend to increase dramatically. With the spread of the Internet and the World Wide Web, with standardized tools, 'web publishing' can bring about dramatic changes in the patterns of knowledge distribution (see Chapter 4).

There are drawbacks, of course. One is *information overload*. This may lead to *information entropy* – that is, the lack of organization and structure. Adept users of these systems rapidly develop strategies for overcoming these drawbacks, sometimes at the price of isolating themselves from new and unexpected information and contacts.[42]

> That there is an over-abundance of information means that the chain from data to information to knowledge has become chaotic. Innumerable actors ('masks') gather myriads of data, which thus are transformed from a potential to a real existence. Data is organized in endless masses of information at all levels, from the infinitely small to the infinitely large. And they are presented to the public with accompanying demands for understanding and action. Information is systematized in innumerable knowledge systems, which are developed from different perspectives and out of different interests. There arises more knowledge than any actor can relate to. And knowledge does not coalesce as a whole. Chaotic masses of fragments arise when a society mirrors itself in thousands of mirrors at the same time. *Therefore, the tools for simplifying are not rational: rationality comes in the plural and is marked by the confusion it intends to transcend.* [translator's emphasis] All actors are struggling on chaotic markets, where they outbid each other's excesses, out-guess each other's guesses and try to know each other's knowledge. In this movement they are pressed into ever more abstraction. But not to wisdom since wisdom transcends and steers clear of the market.[43]

Ways of overcoming information overload become irrational, based on not so clear patterns or reasons of selection. Here are some ways this author has come across, with himself and with colleagues:

- *d)eletion* based on sender: unknown senders or reception of messages as part of a long anonymous chain letter are unceremoniously zapped ('I didn't ask for this junk mail so I am not going to read it').

- *m)ove* excess communications into files for later examination, far down on the priority list ('I'll do it later').
- *f)orward* to someone else for action ('I'm not responsible for this').
- *c)reate* secret mailboxes and email address ('This is for my real communication for a closed circle').
- *a)utomate* my answers. This is what the White House does on its widely publicized BBS ('Let's pretend we're interested').

To put this another way: in cyberspace, everyone has to become his or her own secretary, sorting and filtering the deluge of information pouring in, wave after electronic wave. These few examples illustrate the point that Ole Thyssen is making: that our sorting principles tend to become somewhat irrational in terms of content (but perhaps rational in the sense of survival). Selection becomes preferential and predetermined: some newspapers are not read and some television channels are not watched on principle because I already 'know' that I do not want to waste my time on 'trash'. Choice then becomes based on value, on a perception of the sender as a guarantee for the quality of the information sent. It can also be based on membership in, or identification with, a certain constituency. I subscribe to a certain information source because I subscribe to the values of those who are behind the information. There is nothing strange, or new, about this. The question, which Thyssen addresses, is whether the electronically 'overcrowded room' enhances both fragmentation of meaning and the proliferation of solidified subcultures. He argues convincingly that it does. In an often-quoted passage by T.S. Eliot, the poet asks what happened to the wisdom lost in knowledge and the knowledge lost in information.

As in the realm of material production under capitalism, the problem of cultural overproduction in cyberspace arises.[44] It is not a wasteland, but a jungle grown so thick that all overview is lost. In this thick undergrowth, the power to inform (and to become informed) implies the ability to cut a path. The trails that are staked out also impose meaning. And 'meaning' is to be understood in the sense that 'the manifest exists in the midst of the possible. (And vice-versa.)' The more possibilities, the richer the meaning. This includes symbolic meanings and possibilities.[45]

One effect of ICT, made very visible with the growth of the WWW, is that peripheral, dispersed groups can form communities of interest. The meaning of this globalization of subcultures is probably not yet fully understood. Another effect, easily overlooked because of its simplicity, is the inter-organizational transfer of information. ICT makes it easy to study other organizations' materials, to quote, cut and re-use interesting things. This is automated in the practice of linking websites to each other. Again, the full meaning of this has yet to unfold but a safe prediction would be that this very simple type of inter-organizational transfer and moving about will contribute to the awareness of affinity between organizations. This reflection circles back into the discussions of civil society and self-consciousness of operating in this specific sphere, or these spheres, of human activity.

The social impacts of a technology such as computer-mediated communication have been seen in terms of changes in individual behaviour regarding knowledge, attitudes or actions.[46] Another approach to the social impacts of computer-mediated communication focuses on six aspects: information load, group behaviour, decision-making, productivity, media substitution and organizational structure.[47] The remainder of this study will, hopefully, bring out some variations on an aspect of computer-mediated communication that has been missed in previous studies: the ways in which people are brought together for meaningful action in new ways. In other words, how the use of computer-mediated communication creates networks of people. It should be remembered that our basic linguistic conceptualization of 'networks' and 'networking' is not just the linking of machine to machine, or people to machines, but of linking people to people.

This linking deals with inter-organizational relationships. Two aspects here are especially important. The first is *coordination*. CMC makes coordination of effort possible between organizations. This is more than increasing productivity and efficiency within an organization. There is a synergetic effect, the sum of the effort being greater than the separate efforts of the parts. The second is *discovery*. Computer-mediated communication helps individuals and groups with a common interest to find each other. This aspect of de-isolation may prove to be one of the most important long-term effects of computer-mediated communication.

A final effect will be suggested, that of *agenda autonomy*. Users of CMC, be they individuals, groups or organizations, have the freedom to be heard and to set their own agendas as to what needs to be done. There is no institutional or media filtering. Of the 'thousand flowers' in this wild field many will wither, but many will grow on, nurtured by responses from like-minded people somewhere else, often from unexpected places.

Notes

1. Theodore Roszak, *The Cult of Information*, New York 1986, pp. 136 ff.
2. That this point be emphasized has been suggested by Dr Burkhard Luber, The Threshold Foundation, Germany.
3. Roszak, *The Cult of Information*, p. 138.
4. Ibid.
5. Ibid., p. 141–2.
6. Ibid., pp. 142–3.
7. Bruno Bettelheim, *The Uses of Enchantment. The Meaning and Importance of Fairy Tales*, New York 1977.
8. According to my son, who has written a book on this, the interactive 'live' theater movement in Sweden had by 1997, more active members than the largest political youth organization. See Henrik Soumenin and Tomas Walch, *Saga mot verklighet* (Fairy Tales for Reality), Stockholm 1998.
9. In Steven Levy, *Hackers: Heroes of the Computer Revolution*, New York 1984, p. 431.
10. Lee Felsenstein, 'The Commons of Information', in *Dr Dobb's Journal*, May 1993, pp. 18–24, 20.
11. This was suggested by communications activists at SANGONeT, Johannesburg, at a seminar on a draft of this study in April 1998.
12. APC Charter and Bylaws, posted in <apc.documents>, 5 August 1991 (on APC systems).
13. For an organizational study of the APC, see Susanne Sallin, 'The Association for Communications: A Cooperative Effort to Meet the Information Needs of Non-Governmental Organizations', Progressive Harvard–CIESIN Project of Global Environmental Change Information Policy, 14 February 1994.
14. Ian Peter's 1996 article can be found at <http://www.peg.apc.org/~ianp/welcome.html>.
15. Shelley Preston, 'The 1992 Rio Summit and Beyond', *Swords and Plough-shares*, vol. 3, no. 2, Spring 1994, also online.
16. This section is based on the paper by Barry M. Leiner, Vinton G. Cerf, David D. Clark, Robert E. Kahn, Leonard Kleinrock, Daniel C. Lynch, Jon Postel, Larry G. Roberts and Stephen Wolff, 'A Brief History of the Internet', version 3.1, 20 February 1997, at <http://www.isoc.org/>.

17. *NPR's Morning Edition*, 6 November 1998.

18. David Ronfeldt, 'CYBEROCRACY IS COMING', 1992, at <http://www. cyberocracy.org/cyberocracy.html>

19. Lars Ilshammar and Ola Larsmo, *net.wars*, Smedjebacken 1997, p. 24.

20. *BoardWatch Magazine* is active here.

21. See Leo Fernandez and Somen Chakraborty, 'Social Impact of Information–Communication Technologies', *Social Action*, vol. 48, no. 3, July–September 1998, pp. 253–67.

22. This was pointed out to me by communications activists working at SANGONeT, Johannesburg, during a seminar on a draft of this book in April 1998. SANGONeT is the Southern Africa NGO NETwork, found at <http://www.sn.apc.org>

23. See William Lee Valentine, 'Spreading the Linux Gospel', *PC Magazine*, 8 October 1996.

24. At <http://www.ssc.com/glue/>

25. See Bill Machrone, 'Free-software phenomenon revisited', *PC Week*, 11 November 1996, and 'Linux: Microsoft's real competition?', *PC Week*, 7 October 1996.

26. Glyn Moody, 'The Greatest OS That (N)ever Was', *Wired*, vol. 5, no. 8, August 1997. This article gives a good, non-technical reflection on Linux.

27. Guest editorial by Russell Nelson, 'Open Source Software Model', *Linux Journal*, August 1998, p. 10.

28. John S. Quarterman, *The Matrix: Computer Networks and Conferencing Systems Worldwide*, Bedford MA 1990, p. 21.

29. Ibid., p. 22.

30. Amitai Etzioni, *The Spirit of Community*, New York 1993.

31. Rheingold is not a social historian, nor does he present a political sociology or epistemology. This lapse leads him to believe that the first PC was a Xerox in-house workstation. The whole point of the computer revolution was capturing and spreading the technology from the corporations and the Net from the military.

32. Found at <http://www.rmsd.com/comnet/wwwvl_commnet.html>.

33. Found at <http://php.ucs.indiana.edu/~kgregson/main_menu.html>.

34. Anne Beamish, 'Communities On-Line: Community Based Computer Networks', MIT, February 1995, at <http://alberti.mit.edu/arch/4.207/anneb/thesis/toc.html>.

35. Cyberpunk is defined in the article 'Does the cyberpunk movement represent a political resistance?' at <http://www.clas.ufl.edu/users/seeker1/activism/cybpol.html>. One definition of cyberpunk is roughly what I term 'communication activism'. At <http://www.clas.ufl.edu/users/seeker1/activism/activism.html>

36. 'CYHIST Community Memory: Discussion list on the History of Cyberspace' <CYHIST@SJUVM.STJOHNS.EDU> From: Audrie Krause <akrause@igc.apc.org> 25 August 1996 23:40:03–0700.

37. Mark S. Bonchek, 'Grassroots in Cyberspace: Using Computer Networks to Facilitate Political Participation', The Political Participation Project, MIT Artificial Intelligence Laboratory, Presented at the 53rd Annual Meeting of the Midwest Political Science Association, Chicago IL, on 6 April 1995 (also online).

38. An example near to (my) home is a 'democracy@internet' survey conducted at the Swedish Royal Institute of Technology, dealing with how ICT can support democracy. <http://media.it.kth.se/democracy>

39. See Quarterman, *The Matrix*, p. 128.

40. Ole Thyssen, *Nutiden: Det overyldte rum*, Haslev 1993.

41. See, for example, Mike Sharples and Thea van der Geest (eds), *The New Writing Environment: Writers at Work in a World of Technology*, London 1996.

42. Starr Roxanne Hiltz, and Murray Turoff, 'Structuring Computer-Mediated Communication Systems to Avoid Information Overload', *Communications of the ACM*, vol. 28, no. 7, July 1985, pp. 680–89; Shoshana Zuboff, *In the Age of the Smart Machine: The Future of Work and Power*, New York 1988. See Quarterman, *The Matrix*, pp. 28–9, 43–4, for additional sources.

43. Thyssen, *Nutiden*, p. 121.

44. Ibid., p. 128.

45. Ibid., p. 132.

46. Everett Rogers et al., *Communication Technology: The New Media in Society*, New York 1987, pp. 150–51.

47. Charles W. Stenfield, 'Computer-mediated Communications Systems', *Annual Review of Information Science and Technology*, no. 21, 1986, p. 168.

3

Networking in a War Zone:
The Case of Former Yugoslavia

> Through the example of Sarajevo, the English language came to know a
> new term in the art of war: urbicide.
>
> <http://www.igc.apc.org/balkans/sarajevo.html>

This chapter deals with a specific case of how computer-mediated
communication has been used in a war zone. In 'cyber Bosnia', many
aspects of the emancipatory uses of computer-mediated communication are present. The case presented here illustrates that the Internet is not just fun and games for youngsters and yuppies, or restricted
to ivory-tower academic exchanges, or, more recently, to moving the
shopping mall to our home computer. There are individuals and
groups who are using the new information technology as part of
socially meaningful action. Some of these groups have been around
since the first days of the PC and the beginnings of computer-
mediated communication over telephone lines. Some groups are new
arrivals to the growing global community of communications activists. For these 'netters' the social use of communication and information exchange between groups and across boundaries is
self-evident. However, for many, the Internet and that new frontier
called 'cyberspace) is at once strange, threatening and yet somehow
promising. For some, this new electronic territory, reached by means
of the new info-highways, smacks of escapism.[1]

In the Net

In a *New York Times* article that was syndicated around the world,
American novelist and screenwriter Clancy Sigal described some of
his experiences in 'Cyber Bosnia'.

Today, feeling helpless again as Sarajevo passes its 1000th day of siege, longer even that Leningrad's agony, I have retreated to an imaginary place I call Cyber Bosnia. Only this time it is real. Cyber Bosnia is a cosmopolitan, nondenominational and besieged nation of email users in the former Yugoslavia.[2]

In the midst of warfare, this email user exchanges everyday, human concerns and interests, as well as listening to the tribulations of the besieged. He becomes an intimate witness to the war, in a way more direct than the 'otherness' of watching it on a television that we have raised psychological defence barriers against. Even though Sigal knows of netters involved in rescue and refugee work, the undertone is one of escape. This electronic escape is both for those in Bosnia and for the safeside keytapper who can get away from the collective guilt of a world community that allowed the destruction of one of its members.

There are those, however, who were unable to escape. Most were in Bosnia-Hercegovina. Some fled or were driven away, and yet, in the role of refugee, could not escape being defined by this war. Some chose not to escape and some were caught by their consciences and compelled to act to make Cyber Bosnia not a secret passage away from the war but a way to relieve some of the suffering of the war, hopefully to make a contribution to the end of it. In the following pages, the work of these 'netters' will be presented. They emerge as heroes and heroines of the communications revolution.

From amateur to crisis networking

As Yugoslavia started to disintegrate, or return to its component parts, depending upon your school of history, the threat of armed conflict became more and more vivid. Socially aware netters started efforts to establish an action-oriented computer-mediated communications network in the region. The experiences of those in and around networks such as the Association for Progressive Communications showed that this could be done. When the newly independent Bosnia-Hercegovina was subjected to invasion and insurgency, the need for such a network became more pressing than ever.

In the 1980s countless BBSes (Bulletin Board Systems) sprang up around the globe, more often than not using FidoNet technology. This was also true of Yugoslavia. By the 1990s, there were hopes that a viable 'AdriaNet', a network of small hosts, might have a possible future as an electronic information infrastructure for civil society.

> Some of the existing BBSes in Slovenia, Croatia and Serbia were willing to support the development of a larger network. The existing AdriaNet was to be supported and enlarged....
>
> The first phase began in December 1991 and January 1992. Modems were given to peace groups in Ljubljana, Zagreb, Belgrade and Sarajevo. The connections between the AdriaNet and GreenNet were started. I installed these modems and gave preliminary training to people from different peace groups. The first steps were taken to connect a BBS in Belgrade into the AdriaNet. The AdriaNet introduced two new topic areas for the use of the peace groups.[3]

Like most BBSes of the era there was, however, an amateurish or introverted computerese flavour to many of the systems. Social awareness and social action were not the most distinguishing characteristic. According to one involved netter, 'the AdriaNet is more or less a Slovene–Croat affair'. But the basic problem appeared to be continuity, since BBSes often relied on just one person maintaining the service.[4]

In order to guarantee stable, and boundary-crossing, connectivity to anti-war and humanitarian groups, communications activists began probing possibilities of developing systems with a political profile, such as the PeaceNews in Belgrade, with potentials for local groups for communication and information exchange. Some help was obtained from peace groups in Sweden, the Netherlands, Switzerland and Austria and a communications aid project involving a dozen German peace and humanitarian groups. It was becoming apparent that the peace and humanitarian groups would have to set up their own network in the region. A major obstacle in this type of work was training non-technical peace activists in the use of computer-mediated communication and adapting the technology to their organizational needs.[5]

The Antiwar Campaign in Zagreb and the Center for Antiwar Action in Belgrade decided to set up their own BBS network. In July 1992 the first systems were installed.

> The new BBSs 'ZaMir-ZG' (For Peace – Zagreb) and 'ZaMir-BG' (For Peace – Belgrade) which exchanged mail by way of Austria were now connected with each other and the rest of the world. Letters could be

sent overnight from Zagreb to Belgrade and from Belgrade to Zagreb. Within 12–24 hours letters could be sent and received to and from any other BBS in the APC (Association for Progressive Communications) Network and associated networks. Gateways (connections) to other email networks are also available.[6]

Financial and technical resources were scarce in the beginning for ZaMir Transnational Net (ZTN), and it has only been due to the dedicated work of people like Wam Kat in Zagreb and Eric Bachman (everywhere) that the network survived the early days. External support was organized and systems upgraded, providing stable linkages from the end of 1992. This support is of a varying nature: financial, technical, political, moral. What is perhaps a hallmark of this type of communications activist work is the role of socially aware and committed technicians and netters who 'hack' solutions – that is, improvise and construct solutions to seemingly impossible tasks through a combination of inspiration and perspiration.

The way ZaMir netters solved the problems of communication in war zones is an example of this type of 'better' use of computer-mediated communications. When it became impossible or extremely difficult to maintain direct communication links between the various parts of former Yugoslavia, then relayed links were set up. When it became difficult or not possible to call from Zagreb to Belgrade, then calls were made to a 'node' (station) that could connect to both. Connections have gone through GreenNet in London, LINK-ATU in Vienna, and later BIONIC in Bielefeld, where external funding has helped ZaMir net.[7] Interviewed in a Reuters news release, Rena Tangens, a co-operator of the Bielefeld link, put it this way:

'It sounds crazy to send a message from Serbia to Bielefeld in order to contact someone in Croatia,' she concedes.

But with neighbors once less than an hour's drive apart now divided by battle lines and severed telephone cables, it is for many the only way to communicate. Mail is no alternative. In Bosnia the postal service has broken down, between Serbia and Croatia it is extinct.

'What we have created is the most reliable communication link with and within the former Yugoslavia,' Tangens says.[8]

It is well known that truth is the first casualty of war. This seems to apply even to anti-war activities, and even favourable coverage in the mainstream media sometimes tends to distort. This was pointed out by ZTN activist Eric Bachman, who responded to the Reuters article, correcting the mistakes and readjusting the focus back on the ZTN field workers who were actually doing the work necessary to make the system function. This may be a tendency of mainstream media: to constantly look for singular points of coordination and control and miss the emerging message of CMC – that the network as a whole is its own coordination and control mechanism. Both the full original Reuters release and the comments were posted in the conference <yugo.antiwar> thus making the text available for review and discussion, including feedback to the original authors. Interactive media scrutiny is made possible using computer-mediated communications.[9]

By mid-1993, the Zagreb–Belgrade link was being used by about five hundred users, with thirty-five different groups online. At this time, each of the BBSes sent and/or received about 500 to 2,000 kilobytes a day, which is between 250 and 1,000 pages of text. Messages were both private email and public postings. By mid-1995, there were about 1,500 users on the system.

Users of the ZaMir net were still not charged for the communication services. The local running costs (telephone, electricity) have been covered by the Centre for Antiwar Action in Belgrade and the Antiwar Campaign and Suncokret in Zagreb. Future plans called for raising more funds and spreading the costs among the users.

The ZaMir net had its own conferences which are exchanged between the systems in Zagreb and Belgrade, and elsewhere. Additionally the BBSes offered hundreds of international conferences (from the APC, CL, Z-Netz, T-Netz, Usenet, etc.) which could be read and written to by the users.

> The International Council of Voluntary Agencies (ICVA) an NGO that has a task force for aid to former Yugoslavia has set up its own BBS in Geneva (ICVAGE). Since April 1993 it uses the ZaMir net to have better contact with its member organizations working in Serbia and Croatia. An overlay network of ICVA conferences is now available on ZAMIR-ZG and ZAMIR-BG.[10]

The ZaMir net expanded, adopting the name ZaMir Transnational Net (ZTN). In early 1994 two additional systems joined the network: ZAMIR-LJ in Ljubljana and ZAMIR-SA in Sarajevo. In October 1994 a new system in Pristina (ZANA-PR) became a part of the

ZTN and in early 1995 a station in Tuzla joined.[11] In November 1994, ZTN became a full member of the Association for Progressive Communications; its objectives are congruent with those of the APC.

> The ZaMir Transnational Net aims especially to serve people working for: the prevention of warfare; the elimination of militarism; protection of the environment; the advancement of human rights and the rights of peoples regardless of race, ethnic background, sex or religion or political convictions; the achievement of social and economic justice; women's rights; the elimination of poverty; the promotion of sustainable and equitable development; more and better democratic structures in society, especially the advancement of participatory democracy; nonviolent conflict resolution and to aid the communication between all people, especially for refugees. All groups and individuals who are in agreement with these aims will be actively encouraged to join and use the ZaMir Transnational Net.[12]

What this statement of principle basically says is that the ZTN, like the APC, is there to provide a communications and information infrastructure for groups and individuals trying to make a better world. Some of the content that flows along this infrastructure will now be presented to illustrate the social and political relevance of this type of use of computer-mediated communication.

Content of the ZTN

The ZTN, rooted as it is in the peace movement, is dedicated to maintaining open channels of dialogue between the warring factions and across boundaries. While it does not allow propagandizing or belligerent 'shouting', the ZTN is dedicated to the 'open flow' ideology. This flow takes several different forms within the ZTN and the other info-footpaths into Cyber Bosnia: email, refugee mail services, conferencing, electronic publishing and archive services.

Email for personal contacts and solidarity coordination

With the help of the ZTN email network it has been possible to find and coordinate humanitarian aid for some of the many refugees of the war. It has become an important means of communication for humanitarian organizations working in the war region and sister organizations from other countries. It helps to coordinate the search for volunteers who are helping to reconstruct the damage of the war in all parts of former Yugoslavia. In order to facilitate email exchanges, a 'database' of groups and organizations is being compiled. One volunteer who went for one month to Croatia ended up staying for more than two years. He began to write a daily diary so that his two young sons would later know what their father was doing. This 'Zagreb Diary' was posted regularly in the public APC conference called <yugo.antiwar>.[13] This diary has been distributed widely electronically, reprinted, and some of the proceeds have helped to finance the ZTN.

Refugee mail services

Refugee work was given priority since it soon became evident that computer-mediated communication could both complement and speed up refugee support work of the kind carried on by agencies such as the Red Cross/Red Crescent. Modems were passed around and there were plans to connect laptop computers of relief workers from Suncokret in the refugee camps.[14]

Using connections organized in and around the APC, ZaMir net and the Internet, two refugee mail services collaborated to carry letters for refugees and others in and out of besieged cities in former Yugoslavia. These services are the Sarajevo Pony Express (SPE) and PISMA (Servis za Pisma). The former was a USA-based initative, volunteered by Ed Agro of Boston, Massachusetts, who coordinated the PeaceNet Balkans desk. It thus had its clearing house at PeaceNet/IGC in San Francisco.

> PISMA was developed by a young Serbian refugee who fled to relatives in Belgrade. They both started independently of each other and immediately began cooperating. Both the <*PISMA@zamir-bg.ztn.apc.org*> and the SPE address <*pnbalkans@igc.apc.org*> worked together and independently.... Both worked internationally with volunteers in many countries and with local volunteers (in Serbia, Bosnia etc.).[15]

These services combined computer-mediated communications with fax lines and to-the-door delivery through offline/online relief and peace workers.

> The present situation in this region has resulted in many refugees who are now living in many different parts of the globe. Groups and individuals around the world are helping these refugees by forwarding email for them. Because not everyone has the necessary equipment to use email,

users of the system are offering their support, sending and receiving messages for others. For example, many volunteers in Bosnia are sending and receiving private messages for other people. The messages are destined for friends and family who now live in other widely separated countries. For families that are now separated by even continents, this support is extremely important. Groups have been and are being formed in different countries to transfer email to paper-mail and vice-versa so as to help communication. A group in the Netherlands that is working with the refugees has even been very successful in using email to help reunite families that have become separated as they fled the war zone.[16]

Besides the immediate humanitarian importance of this type of use of email, this type of computer-mediated communication has shown itself to have other long term effects. CMC helps maintain communities in exile through the creation and support for group identity, for internal and external communication and for effective political action.[17]

Communicative interaction through conferencing

A tool for communication and interaction between people using computer-mediated systems like ZTN is conferencing. In an online conference system, an individual can post his or her views, publications and statements. These can then be read and commented upon by other users of the system. That this is a new electronic forum for public discourse and coordination of meaningful action is exemplified by the use of electronic conferencing on the ZTN and connected networks. Some examples of this usage will now be described.

In 1991, the Swedish Peace and Arbitration Society, Sweden's largest and the world's oldest existing peace organization, started directing some of its electronic attention to the Balkan situation. As one of the founders of NordNet, SPAS had access to the APC family of networks and opened an online conference, <yugo.antiwar>, which became something of a communications hub in Cyber Bosnia.

This conference ... was the first international email conference which was opened to deal with working to stop the war here. It now contains the equivalent of 5,000 pages of messages, ideas, opinions, suggestions, actions and discussion about the subject. People from all over the world write to and read this conference. During the last weeks you have people writing about the 'Post-War Views of Refugees', 'Sarajevo Film Days' (Sarajevski filmski dani), the 'Orthodox Peace Appeal', 'Classroom-to-classroom projects', 'Member of Parliament arrested at eviction', 'What after Bosnia', 'Witness' (Svedok), 'The path to normalization' and many more. Authors of the messages come from Switzerland, USA, Croatia, Netherlands, Yugoslavia, Australia, Bosnia & Hercegovina, Germany, Finland and many other countries.[18]

A standing feature in <yugo.antiwar> is Wam Kat's 'Zagreb Diary', a very sensitively written witness to war (see page 88). At the request of aid workers, a special APC conference for refugee work was started, <exyugo.refugee>. The contents deal with aid coordination, appeals and announcements, finding people. One recent coordination effort dealt with the work of an international war resisters' network for aiding resisters to the present Balkan war. Another APC conference <reg.exyugoslavia> contains mainly official documents, press releases from different governments, agencies and organizations. Besides APC conferences, the ZaMir Transnational Net has its own set of conferences.

> '/ZAMIR/!CONTACTS' helps people to find each other, '/ZAMIR/ WHO_IS_WHO' is for users to inform each other about their email addresses. In '/ZAMIR/FORUM' public discussions about any subject take place and '/ZAMIR/PEACE/DISCUSSION' is for peace issues. Some of the media from the Balkan region are beginning to use email to put summaries of their journals on the net. These conferences do have English names, but the main languages of these 'ZaMIR' conferences are the languages of the region.[19]

These examples illustrate that a salient feature of electronic conferencing is its glocality: the subject content can be either local, global or both – simultaneously 'local' and 'global'. Material can be structured by dedicating different conferences to different issue areas. In APC conferences, contributions are usually not anonymous and the 'netiquette' appears more responsible than on other systems such as UseNet. It is the experience of many communications activists that I met during the writing of this book that while conferencing has many advantages and uses, it is still email that tends to draw individuals and groups into computer-mediated communication. In war zones and undemocratic situations, the reasons for this are fairly obvious.

Electronic communication can also play a role in coordinating peace actions. The date 28 January 1995 marked the thousandth day of the siege of Sarajevo. This tragic commemoration was noted and protested against by peace groups in Serbia, Croatia, Bosnia and around the world. Peace and Sarajevo support groups in Belgrade, the capital of Serbia, protested the continuing siege of Sarajevo, even though they themselves had suffered from the international blockade of their country. Here is the beginning of one of the leaflets passed out on the streets of Belgrade:

CITIZENS OF BELGRADE
28TH JANUARY MARKS THE 1000TH DAY OF THE SIEGE
OF SARAJEVO
COME TO THE SQUARE OF THE REPUBLIC ON THAT DAY
AT NOON
Are you aware that during the three years of the siege more grenades
have fallen on Sarajevo than on the entire territory of Yugoslavia
during World War Two?[20]

One of the most important parts of building up an anti-war movement is coordination between groups. This is for the obvious purpose of planning joint activities but also for the equally important psychological effect of knowing that one is not alone. In this respect, computer-mediated communications is a powerful tool. An important observation made by Wam Kat in his Zagreb Diary is that most of the peace work seemed to be done by women.

Media substitution

A major use of computer-mediated communication is for media substitution. This can mean complementing newspapers, radio and television or as an alternative to these often monopolized media. CMC can also be used for distributing and retrieving information that simply cannot be spread or found elsewhere. Volunteers, concerned academics and organizations around the world often gather reports, articles and news, or produce original items, on certain subjects and then forward this material to interested users of email. This method of publishing and/or broadcasting is known as a 'mailing list' (or listmail or listserv). A mailing list is just what the name implies: material is sent out over the Internet as email to a list of electronic subscribers, who automatically get the listserv publication(s) in their emailbox. The material sent out in this way is 'moderated' (controlled) usually from a clearly identified source or sources. In

From Wam Kat's *Zagreb Diary*

17 June 1993 Strange when you look at that whole bunch of groups which has been more or less established out of the anti war campaign have the same significant power structure. All like ARKzin, SunCokret, NeXus, Women Lobby, Women project for Women Victims of War, but also ARK itself and the peace centres in Osijek, Rijeka and Split, as well as the most of SunCokret long term volunteers, are run by or are women. They form not only the majority of the active workers, but also the majority of the decision making bodies. And that's also the case with groups as the Soros Open Foundation and many of the relief organizations I have visited in the last year.

Remarkable when you see that revolution, it is also the first time that I see it happening so clearly, it was not always the case in the countries I visit before. Like Poland, Hungary, the Baltic states and the former CSSR, where after the revolutions also women had a dominate role, but never so strong as here. And it is honestly not so that it could be explained by the war only, that all the men are at the front line, since that is simply not the case. Probably the social researchers will start soon to find out what it is, for me it is women power against a culture which draws on macho beliefs. When the 'old' opposition movement is hooked in endless discussion the new movement 'puts their hands out of sleeves' as we say in Dutch and started to work. They took the risks to get things off the ground. It is, all in all, not a big group, but what has been set up in the last year is unbelievable.

When I was in the town shopping and listening to the stories, that means listening to the words I recognize, I notice that the fighting in Central Bosnia is the talk of the town. In a supermarket a woman was telling a very emotional story about the 'Muslimani', from what I understood it was clear that she didn't really like them. After this I started to wonder were this sudden strong reaction comes from, of course lot's of Croatian people have relatives in BiH and now the Croats are on the run in front of BiH Armija and literally thousands of Croatian refugees are coming down south, that could explain a lot.

Nevertheless if I ask around to find out if there were old histori-cal reasons for hatred between Croats and Muslims, I can't get any clear answer. That is a lot different than for ex. asking about the historical background of the fighting between Croats and Serbs. In that case mostly you get a long historical explanation, going back to the times that Croats and Serbs arrived in this region.

The only real explanation people are giving for this fighting in Central Bosnia is the activities of the both peace freaks Vance and Owen. Their plan to carve up BiH in 10 pieces is seen as the major trigger for this outbreak of violence. Every group started to see each piece as their ethnical part of the country and pushing the other ethnical groups out or place them under their military or civil command. I sometimes have the feeling that they both didn't really foresee the problems they created by coming up with their proposal, I am sure the had all good intentions, but see what happened.

20 June 1993   For the first time in weeks I visited the station today, no special reason, since the days that the station is full with refugees is months ago, just since I had to put Vesna on the tram there. It is also always a good place to watch how new soldiers, boys from maybe just 20 or even younger are brought to the train by their families. It looks as if the soldiers get younger every month....

Just they other day I was talking with another friend who had been in Mostar during the fighting there. He had to be there to visit the family of somebody and give him some news. On his way out he was pinpointed by a sniper who sat somewhere on a roof. He got a safe hiding place behind some pallets full with things that are placed all around the town for hiding. Then the bullets plopped around him into the things on the pallet. He started to get bored after sitting there for about half an hour. So he wanted to know what the 'things' under the plastic were. Especially when one of the bullets had an impact just above his head and some red stuff came out of the plastic. So he took his pocket knife and removed the plastic around the 'things' and who can describe his surprise when he saw tin cans with red beans from America appearing. We heard that some time ago about a hundred tons of food that arrived from the States and that nobody really knew where they went. Now we probably found them again. They are used as shelters on the streets in Mostar.

some systems, the mail lists are put into conferences on a host computer. These 'read only' conferences function then as mail lists but with indexing, which allows a user to choose what he or she wants to 'download' – that is transfer to their own computer.

An example of electronic publishing in Cyber Bosnia is exile magazines such as *Dialogue*.

DIALOGUE started as a media project of Foundation MiZaMir from Amsterdam where war resisters, who flee from former Yugoslavia, are striving to decrease effects of war and hatred and make causes of peace and cooperation. It is dedicated to peace and cultural communication among people from former Yugoslavia, as for the people who stayed in countries formed after decomposing of Yugoslavia, as well as people who sought peace and security in countries of Western Europe. In editorial are present people from all sides involved in fights on the territories of former Yugoslavia. DIALOGUE address to all people of good will who are working on termination of the war, accept nonviolent conflict resolution, active in humanitarian aid or projects for reconciliation and cooperation among people and individuals, as well to people who are looking on these activities with sympathy.[21]

At the beginning of 1995 a digest called the 'South Slavic Mailing Lists Directory' contained the following:

- Bosnet – a moderated, volunteer forum for redistribution of information;
- Croatian-News/Hrvatski-Vjesnik – a moderated, volunteer forum for redistribution of information;
- Cro-News/SCYU-Digest – a non-moderated distribution point (from the WELL) for news;
- CRO-VIEWS – a non-moderated Australian service and an academic level of discussion is encouraged.
- Kuharske Bukve – a weekly Slovene-language cook book;
- MAK-NEWS – two bilingual news services from the University of Buffalo on Macedonia;
- Novice MZT – News of Ministry of Science and Technology of the Republic of Slovenia;
- Oglasna Deska – bulletin board of Usenet type conferences in Slovenia, multi-lingual;
- Pisma Bralcev – an edited (not moderated) mailinglist that provides the possibility of publishing readers' opinions, questions, inquiries for help, answers etc., multilingual;
- RokPress – a moderated mailing-list, intended primarily for news from Slovenia, mainly in Slovene;

- SAGE-net – a moderated group/forum run by student volunteers from the group Students Against GEnocide (SAGE)–Project Bosnia. Its goals are to initiate and coordinate activities among groups active on Bosnia, particularly those on university and college campuses.
- SII – unmoderated network for distribution of news and discussions about the current events in ex-Yu, centered on those involving or affecting Serbs;
- ST-L (Srpska terminologija/Serbian Terminology) – for discussing Serbian terminology for different activities, from terms in Internet to those for culture-bound concepts;
- Vreme – carries 'Vreme News Digest' (selected articles from 'Vreme' translated to English). Since Fall of 1989, 'Vreme' is the major independent newspaper in Yugoslavia and 'neighboring countries'. Since January 1995, by subscription.
- YU-QWest Mejling Lista – unmoderated forum for exiles and emigrants from the territory of the former republic of Yugoslavia.

The above list of electronic sources is surely incomplete at any given point in time and there are numerous other BBSes, lists and sources which dot the info-highway in Cyber Bosnia. Of the fifteen Internet mailing lists presented above, the following source picture unfolds: seven are based in the USA, the UK or Australia (although with much exile input); four are joint Slovene–North American projects; one (MAK-NEWS) appears to be a multinational effort, though with Anglo-Saxon predominance; one is purely Slovene and one purely Serbian, one seems to be Polish-American.

As elsewhere on the Internet, the list servers of Cyber Bosnia are still an Anglo-Saxon affair. It would be most interesting to know how these information services are actually being used, both in the Balkan region and around the globe.

The first service in this list of listservers, Bosnet, presents itself as

a group/forum run by volunteers. Its goals are to present and distribute information relevant to the events in/about Republic of Bosnia-Hercegovina (RB&H); and to initiate and coordinate various initiatives, etc.

The list is moderated, which means that only selected contributions are published. The contributions/opinions presented on Bosnet do not necessarily reflect personal opinions of the moderator or the member(s) of the Editorial Board. To participate in a discussion on a specific topic related to RB&H, please consider Usenet group soc.culture.bosna-herzgvna.

Typical daily posting consists of news briefs compiled from reports by UPI, RFE/RL, NYT, Reuters, as well as numerous other sources, such as: LA, SF, Chicago dailies; WP, WSJ, The Economist, White House, New Republic, Boston Globe, various Ministry Reports, FPB, etc. These postings are in English language.

Bosnet-B: For articles in Bosnian (or Croatian/Serbian) language(s).[23]

When the WWW and Internet began expanding very rapidly after 1994, after the siege of Sarajevo was finally broken, and after the Dayton peace accords started coming into effect, the flow of information and communication, with dedicated lines and all, could increase dramatically (see Webography). Yet one point being made here is that much can be done using only email over normal telephone lines.

Conferences are basically interactive, often with a mixture of sources, and thus function as a forum for communication and debate. For those who want to interact with others – that is, present their own material and/or discuss – then a conferencing system must be used, such as a UseNet conference like <soc.culture.bosnia-herzgvna> or an APC/ZTN conference such as <yugo.antiwar> or several of the mailinglists such as <list.bosnia> (= Bosnet) put into indexed conferences.

One important function of the ZTN is to maintain a flow of alternative news through the publication of materials not found elsewhere. One very important aspect of this is to analyse critically mainstream media, which have played, according to many, a key role in whipping up nationalism and war hysteria in the whole region. One such media watchdog publication is ARKzin, which publishes summaries electronically. This need for media substitution sometimes tends to overshadow the communicative–coordination aspects of global, inter-organizational conferencing, as the two mix in a blend of information, analysis and action.[24]

A major repository for Cyber Bosnia is the 'Balkan gopher' at PeaceNet, part of the Institute for Global Communications in San Francisco. This digital parking lot is available for those who can surf along the Internet. This gopher functions as an online database with the goal of collecting and organizing information on current events in and around the Balkans. For example, it carries a documentation section on war crimes in the territory of former Yugoslavia. The main items here are the bulletins of the Republic of Bosnia-Hercegovina State War Crimes Commission, in several languages.

Click here to see how "big" Bosnia really is.

Road map of Croatia and Bosnia. While following the war in Croatia and Bosnia, did you ever find yourself lost with names like Mrkopalj, Strizivojna, Cvrsnica or Zagonj? I did. And I lived in Croatia for 25 years. Now you can find all and more of those un-pronouncable names on a road map, thanks to Dubravko Kakarigi and his map site.

Cyberbosnia is a group of young people, Bosnian refugees, mainly college students enrolled to various Universities from Norway to Abu Dhabi amd from Turkey to New Zeland. The group is steadily growing. Forward your questions about the life in Bosnia before, during and after the war to that group, and they will discuss your questions and some of them will answer them. It is an exciting new way of making friends.

ZTN support team:

Sarajevo: Kenan Zahirovic

FIGURE 3.1 A clickable map of Bosnia at the Balkans pages, 30 December 1998, <http://balkansnet.org/bosniamap.html> © Ivo Skoric

Cyber Bosnia is growing rapidly and the material produced, gathered and disseminated is of historical importance. Realizing this, an archiving service has started at the University of Essex in the United Kingdom with the task of gathering and cataloguing electronic material from and on the Balkans. In the mid 1990s, when the Internet explosion started, more and more groups and services began using WWW technology. Numerous websites appeared that dealt with the war in Bosnia. And when the siege of Sarajevo was finally lifted, leased-line servers could again come back online from there, for example the Sarajevo Pipeline.

Actors and Spectators in Cyber Bosnia

> All those stories how nice and how good it was in ex-Yugoslavia are fairy-tales of the past. A virtual reality, as the virtual reality that Bosnia was such a peaceful country, (maybe it) was, but it isn't anymore. Wars have left their scars and war is NOT broken houses, it is broken MINDS. Living in a 'war' zone is living in a virtual reality, a reality based on rumors and worries for the future.[25]

One of the 'dangers' of roaming Cyber Bosnia is that the Internet hitchhiker may discover that far from being a 'virtual reality' in the dictionary sense of optical illusion, it is a very real prism, bring reality into focus. In the person-to-person exchanges and through increased information we may gain knowledge and discover that the 'otherness' of what is happening in Bosnia-Hercegovina evaporates when we begin to see that it could very well happen anywhere. Perhaps it is already happening. This is so frightening that we try to maintain the 'otherness', often unconsciously, as exemplified in the following example.

In an article in *BYTE* magazine (March 1995), BIX editor George Bond made a comparison between the increasing narrow-mindedness and policing on the Internet and 'ethnic cleansing' in Bosnia. The inference was that people living in the Balkans must be some kind of barbarians, not like us, since they just go around killing each other. This was broadcast electronically, and so criticized electronically by a Sarajevo computer programmer and analyst. He pointed out that

> Bosnia and Hercegovina is not a dark, faraway place, where people are egoists and xenophobics. It does not consist of some middle-age enclaves

of barbaric tribes.... It did not invent the term ethnic cleansing, it did not engage itself into this practice.... The international court of justice in the Hague, Netherlands, recently used a different term to describe these events in Bosnia, GENOCIDE.[26]

Far from being an escape, a trip to 'cyber Bosnia' can inform and awaken, possibly to meaningful exchange and action with others who are trying to stop a most tragic course of events at the end of our century. As the conflict drags on in the Balkans, flaming up first here and then there, to Kosovo and perhaps elsewhere, the type of work done by the ZaMir Transnational Net becomes ever more necessary. And perhaps not just in the more spectacular events that make the news anyway, but in everyday work of reconciliation: a first step here is communication and finding ways for communication to take place. Unfortunately as this manuscript goes to press, the ZTN is in financial trouble, with external grants terminating and activists unable to fund themselves.

As Dr Burkhard Luber of the Threshold Foundation, Die Schwelle, in Germany has pointed out to this author,

> Zamir is much more than Bosnia and I even – it's a bit bold but ... – may state that the Zamir communication effect for peace groups in Ex-Yugo countries has more profound positive effects in that region than electronic war news releases from besieged Bosnian towns. To formulate it sharply: Zamir did not hinder the slaughtering in the so-called 'free havens' in Bosnia but it did very good work in reconciliation work in conflict areas like E[astern] Slavonia and Baranja.[27]

The challenge of reconciliation and the possible role of computer-mediated communication in this process is constantly being restated. An example is the 1999 tragedy of Kosovo. Can civil society re-construct itself even across the divides of ethnic cleansing? The case study here suggests rather strongly that computer-mediated commu-nication does have a role to play in situations of armed conflict. This role consists of several parts – maintaining dialogue, relief and refu-gee work, and media substitution being major components. The unmediated communication made possible helps to break down the barrier between spectator and actor. This is illustrated in a closing example from the APC conference <yugo.antiwar>.

Bearing witness

Topic 3394 Tuzla Massacre. Eye witness report 26/5/95
2 SRDJAN@ZAMIR-ZG.comlink.apc.org
EYE-WITNESS REPORT OF THE TUZLA MASSACRE

Thursday evening, May 25th, 8.30 p.m. The Day of Youth in former Yugoslavia. Everything has been quiet for more than a week in Tuzla. The weather is perfect: a late spring day, with lots of sun and a nice temperature. A perfect day for a stroll in the old centre of town. Lots of young people meet in this centre: they don't have the money nor the opportunities to do something else. Discotheques are closed, other facilities not available. As always, Kapija is the centre of activity. This old square, that used to be the eastern entrance of Tuzla (how cynical), is filled with people, most of them between 18 and 25 years old. There is no indication whatsoever that a disaster is about to happen. Of course, you can hear the shelling in the distance (Tuzla Airport was hit by 13 grenades), but that is nothing unusual anymore.

Six persons are having Bosnian lessons in the HCA-office, only twenty meters away from Kapija: we want to learn something about Bosnia. Around 9 p.m., there is a big bang. Everybody throws himself at the floor. Panic. Only seconds later, you can hear the screaming, the moaning. People are coming into the office, most of them hysterical. A girl is brought in: she is wounded at her left leg. Fortunately, it is not a severe injury. She's been lucky. But a lot of others were not. Slowly, information is dripping in. A grenade fell in the middle of Kapija. A grenade, fired by the Bosnian Serbs on Mount Majevica, some twenty kilometres east of Tuzla. Don't let anybody tell you something else. Of course, there will be rumours again from the Bosnian Serbs, saying that the Bosnian Muslims did it themselves. Don't believe it: the shellings is the reaction of the Bosnian Serbs to the bombing of Pale by NATO-forces.

A long time it is uncertain how many people have been killed or injured. Ten, maybe even twenty people are killed, and a lot more wounded. But after one and a half hour, when I have gathered enough courage to take a look outside, I can easily see that these are low estimates. Kapija is covered with white sheets, stained with blood, which are used to cover the dead. I count at least forty of them.

I go home, there is nothing I can do. I watch the special programme from TV Tuzla about the shelling. Even my latest estimates are too low. The number of killed people is rising quickly: 45, 50, 53, 60. The shots are awful. Pieces of what once used to be human beings are strewn across Kapija. In the hospital, people are operated upon in corridors, because there is not enough space in the Operation-rooms.

Hundreds of people come to the hospital, hoping to find their children, friends, relatives among the wounded. A lot of them find them among the dead. Fortunately, there are also long cues of people who want to donate blood, to help the wounded.

In the morning, the pain is even worse than in the evening. Slowly realisation comes: a huge part of Tuzla's future, of Bosnia's future, has been killed. TV Tuzla reports 65 deaths, and over a hundred wounded. Almost all of them are between 18 and 25. The city is picking up the pieces. At 8.30 a.m., there is another shelling at Tuzla, but people hardly care: they are still paralysed by yesterday's events. The atmosphere in Tuzla is one of dejection. But even more so, of helplessness. The international community is obviously neither able nor willing to protect Bosnian civilians. The UN-declared 'Safe Areas' are not safe at all. All of them (Sarajevo, Bihac, Zepa, Srebrenica, Gorazde and Tuzla) have witnessed shelling last night, as they have as long as they exist. But the Bosnian Muslims don't have the chance to defend themselves either: the arms-embargo prevents them from buying the weapons to defend themselves. I am not an expert on international law, but I would say that this is against the UN-Charter. Article 51 of the Charter guarantees every sovereign nation the right of self-defence. And Bosnia-Hercegovina is widely recognised as being a sovereign, independent state.

I am not saying that I prefer lifting of the arms-embargo. But the only language that Karadzic and his Bosnian Serbs seem to understand is the language of force. Therefore, the international community should finally take a firm stand. And this means attacking the arms depots of the Bosnian Serbs, not only around Sarajevo, but around all 'Safe Areas'. Even though there might be repercussions on UNPROFOR-troops or civilian targets, it has turned out to be the only way. And if the international community is not willing or able to do this, the only solution is lifting the arms embargo. This would at least give the Bosnian Muslims a fair chance to defend themselves, and maybe it will convince the Bosnian Serbs that they have to find a diplomatic solution. The Bosnian Muslims have more manpower, and if they have the appropriate weapons, they might be able to deter the Bosnian Serbs. The Bosnian Muslims, like most of the other Bosnians, don't want this war. They would like to live again like they have done for centuries: Muslims, Croats and Serbs together, as neighbours, as colleagues, as friends.

The last figures show that there are 68 people killed: a child of two and a half, two persons of 45, and the rest between 18 and 25. Apart from that, there are also 236 people injured. Twenty-nine of them are still in a critical condition. Among the casualties and the wounded of this savage, terrorist attack, all three nations are represented.

Andre Lommen
International Liaison Officer HCA Tuzla
!!

Note for editors: Although I am working for the Helsinki Citizens'
Assembly in Tuzla, this is a personal, and not necessarily HCA's point of
view.
Email: HCA_TUZLA@ZAMIR-TZ.ZTN.APC.ORG

Notes

1. Helpful comments on and corrections to this chapter have been provided by Eric Bachman at BIONIC and Ed Agro at PeaceNet's Balkan
   Gopher (IGC).
2. Clancy Sigal, 'The real Sarajevo is so terrible there has to be a Cyber
   Bosnia', *The Asian Age*, 16 January 1995, reprinted from the *New York
   Times*.
3. Eric Bachman, 'Communications Aid for the Peace Movements in the
   former republics of Yugoslavia, Report, September 1991–May 1993', in
   IGC's Balkans/Ex-Yugoslavia Gopher, (8) ZaMir net, no. 1. Eric Bachman has supplied this author with the whole set of original documentation on the development of the ZaMir Transnational Net (ZTN).
4. <apc.forum> 165.4, 5 January 1992.
5. Joel Sax in <apc.forum> 'Networks in Yugoland', 23 December 1992.
6. Eric Bachman, 'Communications Aid'.
7. Reuters, 'Internet keeps Yugoslavia connected to global village', posted
   in <yugo.antiwar>, Topic 2108, 26 January 1995. As pointed out by Eric
   Bachman in posted comments, Reuters got some of the facts wrong and
   had a slanted perspective.
8. Ibid.
9. Eric Bachman's comments forwarded from ZTN on 2 February 1995.
10. Ibid.
11. Ibid.; ZTN3: ZaMir Transnational Net (Eric Bachman, 11 November
    1994, updated 6 April 1995), correspondence with Eric Bachman, 6 May
    1995.
12. From the ZTN statement of purpose, Version 1.8 1, October 1995 from
    Eric Bachman, 1 December 1998; also ZTN5: Eric Bachman, 'ZANA-
    PR in Wonderland', *KOHA* magazine, November 1994, at <gopher.
    igc.apc.org>.
13. Ibid.
14. Wam Kat at ZAMIR-ZG, 29 November 1992, in <apc.forum> 362.2,
    23 December 1992.
15. Correspondence from Eric Bachman, 1 December 1998.
16. Eric Bachman, quoted from his 'ZANA-PR in Wonderland'; Ed Agro,
    in SPE/PISMA refugee mail services: History and Operation at <gopher.
    igc.apc.org>.
17. See Tiger Li, 'Computer-Mediated Communications and the Chinese

Students in the U.S.', *Information Society*, vol. 7, 1990, pp. 125–37.

18. Eric Bachman, quoted from 'ZANA-PR in Wonderland'; Ed Agro, in SPE/PISMA refugee mail services: History and Operation at <gopher. igc.apc.org>.

19. Ibid.

20. Topic 2106 Belgrade Groups Protest 1000th day 2 responses CAA_ BEOGRAD <yugo.antiwar> 6:03 pm, 26 January 1995, at <ZAMIR-BG.comlink.apc.org>.

21. Topic 215 Introduction to DIALOGUE mizamir yugo.antiwar 2:01 pm Jan 29, 1995 (at antenna.nl)

22. From: Mailing-Lists@KRPAN.ARNES.SI (South Slavic Mailing Lists Directory), in Topic 2092 South-Slav Mailing Lists (Upd) Response 1 of 1 9:00 pm, 14 January 1995, <igc:pnbalkans yugo.antiwar>.

23. Ibid.

24. Cf Wam Kat's comment on this in <yugo.antiwar>, Topic 1773, 7/24/ 94.

25. Wam Kat Topic 2036 Yugoslavs as virtual reality.Response 3 of 4 WAM yugo.antiwar 3:01 pm, 17 December 1994, at <ZAMIR-ZG.comlink. apc.org>.

26. Omer Isak, Topic 533 in <list.bosbia>, from BosNet, 'BosNews', 22 February 1995.

27. Personal correspondence to author, 10 February 1998.

4

Examples of Better Uses
of Electronic Networking

The case of ICT under fire in former Yugoslavia presents a set of concrete uses of how the new technology can be put to work by communications activists in a difficult situation. The present chapter extrapolates from the case of Bosnia and neighbours. Instances that were touched on are exemplified with other but similar uses. The purpose of this is to establish a typology of the emancipatory uses of ICT. Even if some of the categories established are only presented with one or two examples, they represent different *types* of uses. Hopefully, more applications will be found or created as the dialectics of technology and social change continues.

Media Substitution: Bringing Other News to the People

An increasingly noticed use of ICT by communication activists is providing *media substitution* for self-censoring news services, censored either for reasons of the purse or for reasons of the state, or any mix thereof. What used to be known as the 'underground press' has surfaced into the equalizing light of the World Wide Web. But this is with a very important caveat: publishing on the WWW may not prove to be economically feasible in the short run, even if it is a very good way of making a publication known. There seem to be many ways of dealing with this, including advertising, partial publication plus subscription, online publication behind subscribed password protected walls, and so on. Just keeping up with all the WWW sites and mailing lists available around the Internet is a full-time job, as an examination of lists of lists would suggest; for example, <bitl. newlists>, which is a listing of Bitnet lists, or a search-engine search of the WWW and/or Usenet with the keyword 'news'.[1]

It is obvious that the Internet and the WWW have changed the working environment for journalists. Being able to handle the new technology is now mandatory and schools of journalism have not been slow to pick up on this. For investigative journalism, the immediacy of the WWW may mean greater freedom and strength. The types of information described here and below are in no small measure geared to the eyes and ears of these journalists.

What is 'the other news'? Why is it needed when information overload is a growing problem? A first answer is that not all societies are open and that there are still quite a few regimes that openly exercise censorship. Controlling the media is a way of controlling the people. Another answer is that ownership and control of the media in capitalist countries is coming into the hands of fewer and fewer people. And this concentration of ownership is largely in the North.[2] This concentration is reflected in the news services that pick, filter and supply the 'news' to other media before they supply it to the general public. ICT is one way of going around this filtration, of de-mediating the media.

InterPress Service (IPS) started in 1964 as a small news agency run by Italian journalists who wanted to improve reporting about Latin America. It now operates as a syndicated news service, providing articles of depth on events and situations in the South. When IPS decided to go electronic, it signed a distribution contract with the Association for Progressive Communications (APC). Part of the arrangement was that users of APC member networks could access the IPS material after a time delay, so as not to cut into IPS income. In this way, APC users – mainly found in organizations and publications dealing with issues about social change and global solidarity – found themselves with a high-quality flow of information, indexed and databased. Other news services use this type of distribution as well, providing voluntary associations around the world with an infrastructure for the 'other' news.

When government and big media interlock and reinforce each other, the silence can be devastating. An emerging classic in this area is Alex Carey's book *Taking The Risk Out of Democracy: Corporate Propaganda versus Freedom and Liberty*.[3] It was this study that inspired Noam Chomsky and Edward Herman's *Manufacturing Consent*.[4] A theme developed by Noam Chomsky in his writing and speaking deals with the responsibility of writers and intellectuals to tell the truth – not necessarily to the powers that be, for they usually have a pretty good idea of what is happening, but to an informable public that may want to hear the truth and do something about it. But, Chomsky suggests, Western intellectuals have proved to be all too prone to fall into line with the official truths of what Carl Ogelsby once called the Free World Empire while at the same time praising dissidents in undemocratic regimes. In his essay 'Writers and Intellectual Responsibility' Chomsky draws attention to the blacked-out genocide in East Timor. In his view the atrocities there may be the worst since the Holocaust, in proportion to the size of the population; this is being paid for by US taxpayers.[5]

Creating Interaction: East Timor Solidarity

The following is an example of how computer-mediated communication can help groups find each other, exchange information and form coalitions. In early 1991 when I was doing some office work at NordNet, a member of the APC system, I was paid a visit by a young Swede. He was working with a Third World solidarity group. They were interested in our computer-mediated communication system and in getting some more 'alternative' information on a rather obscure area: East Timor, half of an island north of Australia in the Indonesian area. The information was for their bulletin that monitored what was happening. In the wake of decolonization, Indonesia had laid claim, politically and militarily, to East Timor, quelling this country's new independence. A guerrilla war was being waged against Indonesian occupation. The interest of the Swedish group was kindled by the fact of what was seen as dubious arms sales by Sweden to Indonesia, arms that reportedly were being used against the freedom fighters in East Timor.

So, my young Swedish visitor asked if we had any information on East Timor in our system, not really expecting to find any, since he had only rudimentary experience from commercial information-retrieval systems and some amateur BBSes. So we logged on and went to the conferencing system, typing in a keyword search on 'East Timor' and 'Indonesia'. Out came several conferences: one was a newsline service operated by North Americans, another by Australians. Parallel to these conferences for distribution of news were conferences for discussing campaigns and organization. Going to the

Electronic resources on East Timor

Alert mailing list

East Timor Action Network/US has an electronic mailing list for action alerts. These alerts deal with lobbying the US government, severe human rights violations and the like.

Conferences

Reg.easttimor is a conference (newsgroup) that originates from the Association for Progressive Communications (APC) member networks (PeaceNet, GreenNet, Pegasus, etc.). Reg.easttimor contains postings from a wide range of sources, including the National Council of Maubere Resistance (CNRM), ETAN/US, TAPOL, and support groups in Australia, Portugal, Japan, France, Canada, Sweden, England, Ireland, the Philippines, Indonesia, New Zealand and elsewhere. Reports and translations from wire services and the Indonesian, Portuguese, Australian, British, US and Irish press also regularly appear there, as well as official documents and statements from the UN, national governments, and other sources. Postings average 6–10 per day, although the frequency varies with the pace of East Timor-related events. This conference is summarized at ETAN's gopher site and archived, along with much other material, at the University of Lisbon.

This conference and <reg.westpapua> are available by email with read/write access to any Internet address. The APC also has the conference <reg.indonesia> and <act.indonesia> The latter sent out also as a mailinglist. These conferences can be queried by email for their indexes. A particular topic can then be retrieved.

There is a newsgroup on Indonesia-related materials from the world press in both English and Bahasa Indonesia. It is an electronic version of the Kabar dari PIJAR Jaringan Informasi Reformasi newsletter. The Usenet newsgroup <soc.culture.portuguese> includes information on East Timor in both Portuguese and English. The <soc.culture.indonesia> discussion of East Timor is mostly raging debates, with little substantive English-language material not available elsewhere.

Gopher

ETAN maintains background information, including weekly summaries of reg.easttimor, in the Institute for Global Communications Gopher. The URL for this public gopher is <gopher://gopher.igc.apc.org:70/11/peace/timor.gopher>

World Wide Web

East Timor information in English is on the World Wide Web at the University of Lisbon <http://amadeus.inesc.pt/~jota/Timor/> This includes background and current information, and links to many other systems including the IGC Gopher. A record of all UN General Assembly votes on East Timor is at <http://cygnus.ci.uc.pt/~cdpm/votac_e.htm>

Amnesty International's Indonesia and East Timor material is available through <http://www.amnesty.org/> with background material on their 1994–95 campaign in <ftp://ftp.io.org/pub/human-rights/Amnesty/indonesia/>

Source: This is a strongly edited version of the material prepared by the East Timor Action Network, as of April 1997.

---

user register, built in to the APC system, our young Swedish activist could do a global search of users on the system who had registered themselves as being interested in this issue area. Our search branched out and we could also provide my new computer-mediated communication enthusiast with another list of individuals, groups and conferences dealing with the arms trade to the Third World.

This example illustrates several things. First, there is quite often an expectation that the new information technology cannot be used 'progressively': for many the new technology is not part of the solution but part of the problem, to paraphrase Elridge Cleaver. Second, the Swedish group's bulletin on East Timor was provided with more and better information from a variety of sources, increasing this group's effectiveness. Third, and more important, this is an example of how computer-mediated communication helps create human networks: our Swedish activist, and his solidarity group, came into contact with, and became part of, a global community of people committed to stopping an atrocious war. This community of activists has expanded, bringing more and more international attention to this troubled area. The US-based East Timor Action Network is a solidarity organization that also watchdogs developments in West Papua (see pages 107–10). Part of this is lobbying the US Congress on legislation and foreign-policy decisions that affect the area.[6]

A recognition of this work organized in the East Timor Action Network was the awarding of the 1996 Nobel Peace Prize to two people working for peace and human rights in east Timor: Carlos Filipe Ximenes Belo and José Ramos-Horta. The way in which electronic communications is used to support campaigns like the ETAN is illustrated in the listing online of information resources available from the coordination office (see pages 103–4).

Enhancing Interaction: Chinese Students in Exile

The use of computer-mediated communication by Chinese students in the wake of the events of Tiananmen Square in June 1989 illustrates how this technology can be used to strengthen the political position of a specific group. This aspect is analysed in one of the (then) few existing academic studies on the actual uses of computer-mediated communication. The study by Tiger Li, 'Computer-Mediated Communications and the Chinese Students in the U.S.', is found in *Information Society* (vol. 7, 1990). By 1989 there were more than 40,000 Chinese students in the United States, spread out across the country. Two types of computer-mediated communication were being used. One was what is called a 'news group' on the UseNet system (known as conferences or bulletin board postings on other systems). As the name implies, this type is used for broadcasting news. The case in point is an electronic publication known as 'Social Culture China'. According to Li, forty articles per day were being posted here. The other type was computer-based email.

Four types of usage were analysed by Li. First, computer-mediated communication was used as an organizational communication tool. This was important in helping the new Independent Federation of Chinese Students and Scholars (IFCSS) get off the ground and to function as an organization.

> In summary, the CMC system has played a key role in the communication among the Chinese student organizations in the U.S. Without such a

network, the Chinese students who are widely dispersed geographically could not have been organized as a whole to engage successfully in the highly coordinated democratic activities since June 1989.[7]

The second use of computer-mediated communication was that of lobbying campaign tool. The purpose of this campaign was to solicit support for the democratic opposition in China and influence legislators to protect Chinese students. The third use of computer-mediated communication was to provide a public forum for debate on a wide variety of topics. The fourth use of computer-mediated communication was as a news distribution channel.

Did this use of computer-mediated communication by Chinese students make any difference? Li lists four social impacts of the use of computer-mediated communication on Chinese students. The first impact was on group behaviour.

> The major impact the CMC system had on the Chinese students in the U.S. is their transformation from a grouping to a nationally functional group.
>
> Before the CMC system was utilized, the Chinese students in the U.S. were a typical aggregate of people. While they shared some common characteristics, such as the same national origin and student status, they seldom interacted with each other as a whole group, nor did they engage in collective actions aiming at a common goal. The local Chinese student associations that existed before June 1989 were established by the Chinese embassy for administrative purposes. They lacked both interaction and common purposes.
>
> The CMC system helped the Chinese students transform themselves into a functional group....
>
> Needless to say, some social and political events, especially the June 4th Tiananmen Massacre, were the causes that prompted the Chinese students in the U.S. to take collective actions. However, without the CMC system, it would be very difficult, if not impossible, for them to take these collective actions and act as a functional group.[8]

Another impact was on group decision-making. Computer-mediated communication 'provided the most efficient means for the Chinese students to make group decisions. This is best illustrated in their decision to establish a national organization, IFCSS.' Local groups and individuals were brought together, informed and shaped into a community.[9] A further impact is that of media substitution.

One possible impact on the Chinese students concerning media substitution is that for many students, the CMC system may have replaced newspapers as their main source of information about China.[10]

Li reports a survey which found that the electronically distributed *China News Digest* became the major source of information for Chinese students, replacing the official paper, *People's Daily* and other US print (and electronic) media. Did this use of computer-mediated communication make any difference? Li thinks so.

> The study demonstrates that an effective lobby can be implemented by an underfunded citizen group through use of CMC system at a far cheaper cost.
>
> The lobbying experience of the Chinese students shows CMC may be viewed as a citizen technology that can provide social groups with more opportunities to participate directly in the political process. Their experience has the potential to spread to other citizen groups seeking more influence in the political process.[11]

Light in a Blackout: Occupation of West Papua

Many a critic of monopolized mass media have pointed to news blackouts of numerous areas of atrocities and/or Northern incursions into the South. This is both as self-imposed censorship by journalists and as a general pattern of intellectual timidity.[12] One such blind spot is West Papua or Irian Jaya. When the Portuguese and Dutch left their East Indian colonies after the Second World War, the status of several outlying areas was unclear: East Timor and the resource-rich western half of the large island of New Guinea, north of Australia.

> Finally after a thirteen year quarrel between the Indonesian and Dutch governments over the control of what is now Indonesia's 26th province, the issue was decided in 1962 essentially by the Kennedy Government. Known as the 'New York agreement', by which the Dutch-encouraged demands of the West Papuan people for self determination were attempted to be met. However at no point were the local Melanesian population consulted in the process. With vested political and economic interests in the region the U.S government did not want to upset the Indonesian applecart. Resource hungry transnational companies had eager intention to exploit the great mineral wealth that West Papua had within.[13]

The Indonesian military assumed control in 1963 and, six years later, a plebiscite was held on the status of Irian Jaya, in keeping with the international accord. According to one source, only 1,025 voters took part in this referendum that sealed the incorporation of Irian Jaya into Indonesia.[14] Transmigration of the rural population from Java began, as well as exploitation of resources and a repression of opposition. The tribal population of Irian Jaya was being subjected to a cultural and perhaps even physical genocide. The world quickly forgot this war of occupation and displacement of an indigenous Melanesian population, with only very sporadic reports of violence and refugees. Digging out information has been difficult, since the Indonesian government has been very strict on censorship and the governments of other countries such as the USA and Australia have had no interest in rocking the boat of foreign relations or disturbing potentially lucrative areas for business, especially copper and gold mining. Several western countries and the World Bank have continuously supplied Indonesia with aid and arms.

Resistance to the Indonesian occupation and transmigration started in the 1960s.

> At the forefront of the armed struggle for a free West Papua is the Organisasi Papua Merdeka, the OPM. Indeed the OPM is as much a collective state of mind within most dispossessed West Papuans, as it is a body of militant men. The OPM has been active ever since Indonesia took over from the Dutch in 1963/64. Neither Indonesia nor PNG formally recognizes the OPM. Its force as a liberation movement has been diminished with factional infighting over the years but in the recent past a younger new order OPM with cohesion and strong leadership has emerged.[15]

Perhaps due to the expansion of mining activities and the increase in visibility and information that this entails (shareholders in mining companies such as Freeport want to know where their money is going), there is a growing international interest in West Papua. Groups interested in human rights and indigenous peoples started focusing in, organizing and networking with each other. A natural starting point was to tie in to the work of the East Timor solidarity movement. Computer-mediated communication in its various forms became a powerful tool.

In November 1996, the following message was sent around the Net, announcing the WWW site of the OPM liberation movement:

> On behalf of Moses Werror, Chairman of the OPMRC (Organisation for West Papuan Independence), boyjah would like to announce the launch

of the following URL to the West Papua Niugini/Irian Jaya homepage. Please check it out and use it to help us in our fight for freedom. http://www.twics.com/~boyjah/westpapua/humanrights.html
One People one Soul   boyjah.[16]

On 20 September 1997 this author listened to a report on BBC World Service about this site and the situation in West Papua. When my first check around the WWW did not produce any results, I contacted the BBC. After some digging around in transcripts, they came up with the URL listed above. But a week after the BBC report, the OPMRC site was gone. Two months later, it was still being listed on WWW search engines, but was off its server in Japan. What happened? My first inquiry at the host (TWICS) did not result in any information. A renewed questioning also gave no information.[17]

An 'information kit' on West Papua was put together in 1995 by the Australia West Papua Association in Sydney and made available online.[18] This kit is an online book covering West Papua and human rights issues. An excerpt from the introduction reads as follows:

> The displacement of tribal groups through the government and World Bank sponsored Transmigration program, the uncontrolled logging of the country's forest resources, and the massive extension of the Freeport mining concession area by 2.6 million hectares will continue to degrade the environment and the indigenous peoples of West Papua. A recent wave of killings and acts of intimidation by members of the Indonesian armed forces and Freeport security heralds an upsurge in the level of repression against the West Papuan community. The Australian Council For Overseas Aid (ACFOA) has recently issued a report (April 1995) titled 'Trouble at Freeport' which documents eye witness accounts of current Indonesian military repression, and assesses the social situation. It was a situation described by ACFOA as being so fragile as to have the potential to 'go off like a time bomb unless legitimate rights and grievances were quickly and responsibly addressed'. The comparison drawn with Bougainville highlights the desperate nature of the problem.

Another use of the WWW is for 'news watch' siting. In this type of activity, news stories are picked up and reposted in thematic areas. Over time, subject archives can be accumulated for research, in-depth journalism and solidarity work. One such site that picks up information on West Papua is maintained by people at Journalism Studies, University of Papua New Guinea, at <http://www.pactok. net.au/docs/nius/>.

APC networks carry a pivotal conference <reg.westpapua> that functions as a clearing house for activist information and for coordination of activities. Started in 1995, this conference has contributors from around the world, reflecting the global character of the solidarity movement. The United Nations has rules and procedures for dealing with decolonialization. One goal of the solidarity movement is to put the issue back on the agenda of the United Nations, since the terms of the New York Agreement may not have been fulfilled.[19] Whether this will succeed is an open question.

Boundary Bashing: The Electronic Perforation of the USSR

When he first opened the Soviet Union's media to dissenting ideas in the mid-1980s, Mikhail Gorbachov could not have predicted the ultimate impact. To the surprise of the world, and of Gorbachov himself, his policy of *glasnost* helped dissolve one of the most powerful empires in modern times. The explosive change was triggered by millions of people hearing alternative ideas, among them ideas that resonated powerfully with their private feelings....

With the country suddenly flooded with free criticism and new public ideas, millions of formerly passive Soviet citizens saw their private desires legitimated by reflection in the mass media. It was that legitimation that helped bring an end to the old Soviet empire.

Ben H. Bagdikian, *The Media Monopoly*

One important aspect of computer-mediated communication is its disrespect for boundaries. This aspect became clear in the role played by electronic communications networks in the democratization process in eastern Europe and elsewhere. Of course, radio and especially television have been the most important media here, as demonstrated by the spontaneous defence of television transmitters by unarmed civilians in Romania, the Baltic countries and Russia. Here are some examples which show, it is hoped, that the penetration of the Soviet empire by 'the media', while important – perhaps crucial – in its downfall, did not just 'happen' (see pages 114–15). There was more to this penetration than met the eye. The release of the 386 chip, which made CMC systems viable at low and portable costs, for export to the USSR, and the setting up of the San Francisco–Moscow teleport, were important steps toward electronic perforation.

In the Baltic countries 1991 started with a 'black January'. The Soviets were putting last-ditch military pressure on these countries, in the form of special 'black beret' units, to coerce them to remain within the Union. Unarmed civilians raised human and stone barricades around their parliaments and television stations in Tallinn, Riga and Vilnius. While these television stations (and foreign television teams) were showing pictures of a diminutive number of guards armed with shotguns in parliaments in the capitals of the Baltic states, what they did not show, probably because they were not supposed to know, was that the parliaments were running clandestine computer-mediated communication systems and broadcasting information out to the world via the matrix. In computer jargon, this 'Baltic link' was a communications 'back-up' system, also used for international liaison.

The Baltic link developed out of communications work carried out before, during and after the 1990 END (European Nuclear Disarmament) conference. As part of the new thaw in the Cold War toward the end of the 1980s, with *glasnost* and détente, it was decided that the 1990 END conference would, for the first time, be held in the Soviet bloc. This was a peace propaganda feather in the political hat of the new Soviet leadership and not without controversy within the Western peace movement. So the compromise worked out was that half the conference would be held in Helsinki, Finland, and the other half in Tallinn, Estonia, just a few hours by ferry across the Bay of Finland. A computer-mediated communication system, connected to the APC system, was established in order to do the necessary informational work around the END conference.

In the Autumn of 1989, the telephone exchange in Tallinn began modernizing, installing sixteen automatic exchange lines across the bay to Helsinki. This technical modernization was crucial. In a manually operated system (for foreign calls), it is easy to pull the plug as well as monitor. This control is more difficult in an automatic system. This 'hole' in the Soviet telephone system was soon discovered and used not only by the peace movement, but by amateur BBS 'hackers' around the globe. Due to the anomalies of the Soviet telephone system, it was easier, provided one had access to a special international line in Tallinn, to call Stockholm and London than Tartu, Estonia's second largest city. In order to organize the END conference, an international telephone line was made available, which the peace movement had access to. The computer-mediated communication system set up in Tallinn for the END work was soon relaying communications from all over the Soviet Union, especially around the Baltic basin, out onto the matrix, mostly via the APC nodes NordNet (then PeaceNet/Sweden) in Sweden and GreenNet in Britain. This set-up survived the END conference, was developed and refined, with more equipment, such as modems, being smuggled in (by this author). So when the political crackdown came in the Baltics in early 1991, and the showdown in Moscow in August 1991, the Soviet communications system had been penetrated in such a way that it proved impossible to patch up the holes. An important part of this was that a relayed, decentralized computer-mediated communication system becomes invisible. In the case at hand, it appeared that a computer-mediated communication user in (then) Leningrad was making a domestic call, when in fact 'online-frontline' news was being relayed out onto the global matrix (See pages 114–15).

> Fortunately, we do have at least some positive things to tell about the performance of GreenNet, PeaceNet, PopTel etc. during the Soviet August Revolution. First, we continued to receive email from members of the Golubka peace team, who use the new GlasNet node in Moscow. Thus, we were able to follow the day-to-day actions and feelings of the 'golubkis' even in this situation of emergency.
>
> Secondly, PeaceNet-Sweden (the Stockholm node within the APC system) brought the news stories from 'Severo –Zapad' (NorthWest), an independent news agency on environmental, economical and political developments in the Northern and Western regions of Russia (and the Baltic Republics) working in Saint Petersburg/Leningrad in close co-operation with green and environmental movements. The conference <northwest.news> on PeaceNet-Sweden is now updated daily via the DIX-computer in Tallinn (see Interdoc Newsletter 3, April 1991 for background details).
>
> A leading 'serious' British newspaper (the *Independent*) actually ran a large article a few days after the end of the coup saying what an important role the private computer networks had played in spreading news of the coup. The article implied that the journalists at the *Independent* had made good use of material available on bulletin boards in the USSR at the time of the coup. The article implies that the author had also read the items written by North West News. So maybe some of the mass media was actually using the same sources that we were looking at.[20]

Of course, foreign and other journalists and established news services can do this, but it is easier to exercise censorship here, round people up and pull the plugs than in a decentralized system. In the case of the Moscow coup attempt, this did not happen to any great

Barricades at the Estonian parliament in Tallinn, early 1991
(*J. Walch*)

North West Agency Report, Saint Petersburg, 21 August 1991

This Day (August 19) we just went to our job. Editors, who were on duty not yet believing it had happened, began to call our outside correspondents and connect with the mass media. Those of us who had been at home began to appear in publishing houses and to get together. Our mood was of alarm. One of our colleagues came warmly dressed as if it was October outside. It turned out that he had thought he would have to spend the night in jail.

By 1.00 p.m. that day it was clear that the Russian government and municipal authorities of Saint Petersburg intended to resist the junta. We didn't know at that time that we were the only information agency still operating in the city with international and trunk communications. In the early morning local putschers destroyed the telephone network, faxes and computers in the city by broadcasting a strong electromagnetic impulse. Our equipment remained working only because we have had a lot of experience of working in the independent press. We had already switched off and removed all working equipment.

We picked up and distributed all the city newspapers without permission. All the editors refused to publish their papers under the conditions imposed on them. 'Vecherny Leningrad' (Evening Leningrad) was issued with blank spots on the front page. On TV net stooges of junta were reading for the hundredth time the junta's 'decree'. Leningrad radio was silent.

On August 20 two independent radio stations 'Radio Baltica' and 'Otkrytyi gorod' (Open city) started to broadcast on the medium wave from one transmitter located outside the city. For two days and nights the radio journalists didn't leave, having become the resistance's voice.

Our agency was in fact the only source of information for them. 'North-West' agency journalists were literally shouting across defective lines hot information from the Leningrad and Moscow city councils, the 'White House' (the building of Russian Supreme Council), and from the square in front of the Mariinsky Palace (the city council building) which was surrounded by 3–4 rows of a living barricade.

At 0.05 a.m. the Russian Information Agency announced the storming of the 'White House'. The city didn't know yet. While we had been phoning the radio station, fax-machines were releasing a hastily written sheet of paper: 'According to Supreme Soviet of the Russian Republic the erection of barricades has begun near 'White house'.

The first line of barricades has been overcome there, and we can hear the first shots and bursts of machine-gun fire. The storming of the White House's begins.'

We could imagine what was happening at that moment to many Leningrader's families and we were extremely upset both for them and for ourselves. It was at that time that the thunderstorm of tank fire started on Nevsky prospect. At 2.00 a.m. city vice-mayor Vyacheslav Shcherbakov and fleet commander counter admiral Chernavin declared on the radio that Baltic fleet sailors and military servicemen of Leningrad and its district supported the legal government.

Our old fax-apparatus was hot, our fax-paper supply was running out. We feared most of all that our only computer would break down because of the tension!

There was another threat: in Tallinn, Estonia strategically important objects were being stormed. At any moment troops loyal to the junta could seize the telephone station with which we were communicating to the world with the aid of our computer. Our correspondents having been near the Mariinsky palace and at the city council informed us that the barricades around the palace were growing and a great deal of people were moving toward Isaac square. All approaches to the palace were guarded by Afghan veterans and OMON (Interior troops) employees. At the entrance to our building were six Afghan veterans on duty from a local 'Decembrist' club.

All the workers gathered at the agency, journalists, programmers and messengers, gathering and sharing news. Inhabitants of nearby houses visited us and brought food and coffee. At 2.00 a.m. we got and transmitted to the whole city, council chairman Alexander Belyaev's hand written appeal. At that time tanks were about 70 kilometres from the city, and in Moscow it appeared that people had been killed and wounded. This was a terrible fact for everybody to hear. But we overcame and for the first time in 74 years it was clear we had won.

By the morning of August 21 we were collecting all the sheets of paper, documents, and summaries that would go into historical archives and museums.

Contact details about NorthWest:'Severo-Zapad' (North-West) Information Agency,
Editor-in-Chief, Elena Zelinskaya, Computers & Communications' Dept.
Director, Roman Ignatiev, Tel. (+7–812) 310–0596,
Fax: (+7–812) 310–7329, Email: INTERNET: NortWest@p2013.f20.n490.z2.
Fidonet.org   UUCP: FUUG!CASINO!490!20.2013!NORTHWEST; APC: dix:northwest

extent, and Mikhail Gorbachov even commented later that he relied on the BBC to find out what was happening. Of course, in a coup situation, isolating one's own population from coordinated resistance is the primary goal, not foreign news coverage.

While Soviet power was putting the thumbscrews on the Baltic countries in January 1991, the 'allies' were waging war against Iraq. As analysed in several studies, this war was a television war and news was highly controlled and censored. A Finnish netweaver, Mika Böök, writes on this in InterDoc Europe:

> Earlier this year, the international network for computer conferencing and email brought a positive surprise to its members, the users. Thanks to the combined efforts of salaried staff (of the computer networks themselves, and of some of the participating organizations) and of voluntary groups and active private citizens (of various countries) the Middle East conferences of the PeaceNet succeeded in providing a veritable day-to-day 'coverage' of the events of the Gulf War, and of the movement against the war that developed in the USA and in Europe. In the crucial months before, during and after the war the computer system became a true alternative (i.e. uncensored and critical) information service.[21]

There seems to be enough evidence to conclude that the electronic perforation of the Soviet Bloc either contributed to its downfall or was at least a companion to the process of democratization. The spread of ICT does not bring down dictatorships but it can support groups and individuals working for the open type of society necessary for democracy.[22] One person who believes that the electronic perforation of the Soviet bloc helped in its downfall is Hungarian-born billionaire George Soros. He has financed organizations and computer networks with the goal of furthering the open society. His philanthropic efforts in supporting programmes for bolstering civil society, including electronic networking, in eastern Europe have not been without their critics. For some, the opening of closed societies by big capitalists is seen as opening the door for hamburger culture and foreign exploitation. Given his track record of moneymaking on the currency markets, Soros was open to this type of criticism. Yet he has also come out in heavy criticism of unfettered global capitalism as the biggest threat in the world today. One is reminded of similar criticisms of the philanthropy of nineteenth-century 'robber baron' Andrew Carnegie. Whatever Carnegie's motives, many of his

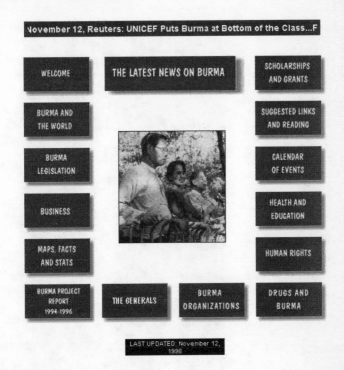

FIGURE 4.1   Burma Project homepage <http://www.soros.org/burma.html>

"ပျော်ရွှင်သော
မွေးနေ့ဖြစ်ပါစေ"

နေအိမ်အတွင်း
အကျဉ်းချနေ
ရတဲ့ (၆)နှစ်တာ
ကာလအတွင်း
ဒေါ်အောင်ဆန်းစု
ကြည်ရဲ့ ကိုယ်
ကျိုးစွန့်အနစ်နာ
ခံမှုကို ဂုဏ်ပြု
လေးစားတဲ့အနေ
နဲ့ဒေါ်အောင်ဆန်း
စုကြည် နှစ် ၅၀
မြောက်မွေးနေ့မှာ
အပြည်ပြည်ကိုင်များ
အောင်းင်းလိုက်
ပါတယ်။
ဒေါ်အောင်ဆန်း
စုကြည်အမြန်ဆုံး
ပြန်လည်လွှတ်
မြှောက်ပြီး မြန်မာ
ပြည်ငြိမ်းချမ်းရေး
နဲ့ ဒီမိုကရေစီ
အမြန်ဆုံး
ရရှိပါစေ။

SET HER FREE!

THE 1991 NOBEL PEACE PRIZE WINNER

6 YEARS UNDER HOUSE ARREST

AUNG SAN SUU KYI'S 50TH BIRTHDAY

International campaign in support of Aung San Suu Kyi, 1995

public libraries have outlasted his steel mills. Soros's Open Society Institute finances websites, including one called 'The Burma Project' (see Figure 4.1).[23]

A very closed country, Burma was by the late 1990s under heavy electronic surveillance. This is being done in several ways: by bringing information out of Burma to the world on what is happening and thereby creating a public awareness of the repression going on and hopefully persuading politicians and businessmen to put economic and political pressure on the regime, and to aid refugees; and by facilitating the organization and coordination of resistance to repression, giving support to movements for democracy, organizing a world-wide boycott, protesting ASEAN support to the Burmese dictatorship, and so on. The spreading of information, including the gathering and reposting of mainstream news, is done on several websites such as FreeBurma, BurmaNet and the Burma Project site mentioned above. The Free Burma Coalition site is, as the name suggests, a coordination point. These websitings are fairly sophisticated. For example, the Free Burma site offers not only printed materials but also pictures, slide shows, sound and video clips from Aung San Suu Kyi, Nobel Peace Prize laureate and leader of the opposition front, the National League for Democracy, as well as rebroadcasts from Radio Free Burma. A major source of information is the *BurmaNet News*, distributed in a variety of electronic ways.

Since modems are illegal in Burma, email penetration is low. In April 1997, Burma established its first leased computer link with the outside world, a 64kbps packet switching line to Singapore. A rueful comment in the electronic conference <reg.burma> was: 'The only catch is that you could go to jail for 3 to 5 years if you are caught with a computer and a modem which effectively gives you zero-bandwidth.'[24] A focal point for the inter-organizational discourse and exchange is <reg.burma>. Started in 1993, this conference archives an enormous amount of material on the struggle for a democratic Burma (see Figure 4.1).

Bypassing Hierarchy: NAN and a Nobel Peace Prize

An important aspect of computer-mediated communication is that its use is empowering. Individuals and groups can gain a wealth of information, communicate around common interests, and coordinate

actions. 'Bypassing hierarchy' means not only the obvious circumvention of commercial and state hierarchies, but to no mean degree
the circumvention of organizational and decisional hierarchies within
organizations. In terms of organizational analysis, it is horizontal, or
lateral, communication at the expense of vertical communication.
Often, the hierarchy is simply ignored. Instead, cross-organizational
ad hoc coalitions are formed to deal with a specific task.

The 1980s witnessed 'the last hooray' (we hope) for the superpower arms race. Part of the 'forward positioning' strategy of the
United States was to place short- and medium-range nuclear missiles
in central Europe – a clear signal of where the next battlefield was
going to be. This triggered the European Nuclear Disarmament
(END) movement. Another part of this US strategy was to move the
North Atlantic defence perimeter further up the Norwegian and
Greenland coasts. This was to contain an increasingly active Soviet
nuclear fleet and military activity in the far north. The response of
the peace movement to this was the creation of North Atlantic
Network (NAN), with the purpose of monitoring superpower
activities, spreading information about this and coordinating protest
activities. Much of NAN's coordination took place via computer-
mediated communication. A focus of organizing protest was both
the home-porting of nuclear vessels and visits by nuclear-armed and
-powered warships, visits to ports that were nuclear-free, either by
law or by political policy. NATO's waving of the nuclear umbrella
above the heads of many who did not want it became a politically
inflamed issue in many countries – many local town councils banned
such visits. New Zealand barred all nuclear vessels from its waters
and was declared *enfant terrible* by the United States. The use of
computer-mediated communication was especially suitable for the
quick kind of multilateral, global coordination called for in putting
together this type of anti-nuclear coalition.

Another example of non-hierarchical networking, assisted through
CMC, is the International Campaign to Ban Landmines (ICBL).
Some 26,000 people are killed or maimed every year by landmines.
These anti-personnel (AP) mines stay around long after the soldiers
and wars are gone. So most victims are civilians, many children.
Removing the landmines is costly and difficult, so countries in the
Third World have to live, or rather die, with these 'quiet killers'.
One good way of getting rid of landmines is to stop producing

them. So in 1991, Vermont activist Jody Williams took the initiative for the ICBL. The campaign is an example of 'peoples' pushing': there was a 1980 convention on landmines; the United Nations had in various ways been involved in the issue, as had other international organizations. But it was when the campaign gained momentum in the mid-1990s that the issue of a total ban on anti-personnel land-mines was put, and kept, on the international diplomatic agenda. When the ban treaty was agreed upon in September 1997, the campaign had a thousand member organizations around the world. A month later, the 1997 Nobel Peace Prize was awarded to Jody Williams and the International Campaign to Ban Landmines. As mentioned earlier, Carl von Essen, a member of the ICBL board, voiced the opinion that the campaign had won the Prize because it was an effective, non-hierarchical organization thanks to electronic communications.[25]

How do electronic communications enable organizations like the ICBL to succeed? The following factors are important. Internal coordination is facilitated thanks to electronic communications such as email and conferencing, as well as distribution of internal campaign materials. For example, the ICBL steering committee members are linked through email. In distributed, electronic confer-ences such as <disarm.landmines> found on APC networks, members and supporters of the campaign can exchange informa-tion, discuss this information and coordinate activities. All this self-organizing and coordination can be done in a transparent way that does not use any organizational or informational hierarchies. This type of network organizing diminishes the need for central co-ordination and administration and must be seen as a clear way of increasing effectiveness.

External exposure is optimized. Using WWW technology, inter-ested individuals – and, above all, journalists in print and electronic media – can find full documentation in an easy manner. One of the founding members of the ICBL, the Vietnam Veterans of America Foundation, has maintained a professional 'show-site' for the ICBL, with up-to-date information as well as background information on the issue at hand (landmines), with a history of the campaign itself, who belongs, and links to other websites – in other words, every-thing a journalist needs for making a story (found at <http://www.vvaf.org>).

Campaign for a
LANDMINE FREE WORLD

Turning Tragedy Into Hope

♦ *US Campaign*
♦ *International Campaign*

🏠
home

In 1990 Yor Piriy stepped on a landmine on her way to sell food. This tragedy transformed her life forever: She was rushed to a hospital at a refugee center where both of her legs were amputated. In Cambodia, a combination of religious and cultural beliefs conspire to leave the disabled ostracized and shunned by their communities.

During her recuperation, Yor lost hope for the future and tried to commit suicide. Piriy and her husband were separated; she has not seen him since then and believes that he has remarried. She was unable to find work after leaving the hospital and lived with her mother and two sisters. "In my mind," she said, "I was a problem. They had to do everything for me."

FIGURE 4.2   ICBL homepage <http://www.vvaf.org/landmine/>

This is not enough, however, to bring about the signing of an international treaty. It was the Canadian government that took the negotiations out of the UN system when the issue of AP landmines fell off the effective agenda in the disarmament talks.[26] But this initiative was also the result of a global campaign that kept the issue on the public agenda and kept the discourse alive. And it should be realized that countries like the USA, Russia, China and India are opposed to the ban treaty as it was signed in December 1997 in Ottawa. This aspect of *agenda lobbying* by associations is strengthened through ICT.

The fact that the Norwegian People's Aid was, according to itself, 'the world's largest humanitarian mine clearance organization' probably influenced the choice of Oslo as the venue for working out the treaty.[27] A result was the announcement of Norway's intention to start clearing out its (NATO) landmines, which brought a protest from the US government. Campaigns against arms manufacturers started to take effect. Swedish Bofors announced in December 1993 that it would terminate production of AP landmines.[28] Something was happening.

Crisis Communications: B92 and Student Protest 96 in Belgrade

Given the course of political events in central and eastern Europe since *glasnost*, it is not unreasonable to take a democratization perspective in the analysis and interpretation of recent history in this corner of the world. For the long struggles of Solidarity in Poland, of dissidents in Leipzig, velvet revolutionaries in Czechoslovakia, in Hungary, in the Baltic states and in Russia have changed not only the political map of Europe but also how the history of the continent is being perceived.[29] What can be seen if we take this perspective – the flow of democracy – to Yugoslavia? The break-up of the Yugoslavian federation meant, among many things, a weakening of the hold of the Communist Party elite. This opened the door for democratization. The disintegration into civil war may have been aided by elites' attempts to block the unseating of autocratic apparatchiks left over from the days of one-party dictatorship (but with new ideological labels). The demonstrations and protests in Croatia and Serbia were quelled and demands for democratization were pushed aside in the frenzy of the war in Bosnia. From this perspective, it is not surprising that soon after the Dayton Accords imposing a ceasefire between the warring sides in Bosnia, demands for democratization should surface again.

On 22 November 1996, students in Belgrade began demonstrating in protest against attempts by the socialist regime to hijack the local elections in Belgrade, won by parties in opposition to the Milosevic government. After four days of protest, the Head Committee of the *Student Protest of '96* approved the following declaration:

Declaration of Decency

We, the students of The Belgrade University, support the citizens of Serbia who demand protection of their guaranteed Constitutional rights. A brutal violation of law and annihilation of the regular electoral results are an unprecedented attack on the basic principles of democracy. We are not taking sides between the party in power and the opposition – what we insist upon is the rule of the law. Any government which is not willing to acknowledge its own electoral defeat does not deserve our support and we overtly oppose it.

Therefore, we demand:

1. An immediate establishment of a Governmental Electoral Committee which would be formed on the principle of proportion between parties that took part in the second round of voting. The purpose of the Committee is an objective establishment of the outcome of the second round of voting.
2. A resignation of the Chancellor of The Belgrade University, prof. Dragutin Velickovic because of his ignorance of our protest and our demands. His communication with the students based on orders and interdictions is not acceptable.
3. A resignation of the student-vice-chancellor of the Belgrade University, Vojin Djurdjevic, who no more represents the students, but the party in power.

We appeal on all the participants of the current political crisis to abstain from any violence. The students of The Belgrade University will endure in their protest.[30]

And endure they did. Daily student demonstrations were held in Belgrade. A target of protest was the state-controlled media: newspapers such as *Politika*, radio and television stations. The divided opposition parties began to close ranks and took to the streets in demonstrations taking place immediately after those of the students. A daily routine developed, gathering about 10,000 people day after day, even in rain, cold and snow. After two weeks of demonstrations, protests began in other cities in Serbia. Some cracks in the regime began to show: for example, judges began publicly questioning the legality of the government's reversal of local election results, and the Socialist Party leader in the city of Nis resigned.[31]

The Serbian government got nervous and closed down the student free radio station B92 (Belgrade at 92.5 MHz). 'Free' here means non-state. Perhaps the Serbian government thought it could get away with this, as did the Croatian government in early 1995 when it closed down independent radio there.[32] But 200,000 people came out into the Belgrade streets in peaceful demonstrations in protest against this censorship move by the government. This would eventually prove to be self-defeating, since the Serbian government was facing not only mass student demands for democracy but also a coalescing front of opposition parties asserting what they saw as their legal right to office in Belgrade, as well as an increasingly irate media.

Even before the events in November 1996 the students had taken to the Internet to organize international support for their demands for democracy. Using email, lists and the WWW, with support from networks such as the ZTN, their struggle was already known in activist circles. As their protests picked up, the students found increasing international support. For example, their website was 'mirrored' on other sites in Europe and the USA, easing access for Internet users.

The Serbian government must have been poorly informed about the state of WWW technology. For when the B92 radio station was closed down on 5 December, transmissions continued via the Internet. This technology had been around for a while, but was becoming more and more popular thanks to software packages that could be freely downloaded into PCs and then used for listening to audio, and watching video either streamed over the Internet or downloaded into a PC (B92 used the 'Real Audio' package from RealNetworks). The Voice of America rebroadcast B92 programmes back into Serbia on short-wave. The corporate media picked up on the protests, both through their 'normal' channels (newsprint, radio and television) and the 'new' channels offered on the WWW. After a few days, the Serbian government backed down. Parallel to this, the Croatian government had been trying to close down the independent Radio 101 in Zagreb, but also backed off in the face of protests and retransmissions over the WWW.[33] When politicians challenge the media, they of course

SRPSKI

FROM THE B2-92 NEWSROOM

Serb war crime suspects arrested
German KFOR troops in the Kosovo town of
Orahovac have arrested three Serbs suspected of
committing war crimes. The Hague Tribunal denies
involvement...▸▸

Andjelkovic: UN's job is not to relocate Serbs
Kosovo Council head Zoran Andjelkovic today
reacted angrily to a suggestion that the UN
Mission in Kosovo may relocate Kosovo Serbs to
"safe areas"...▸▸

Draskovic overshadows opposition rally
Sometime regime partner Vuk Draskovic's
"surprise" appearance at last night's opposition
rally in Belgrade dominated the event...▸▸

Rally organisers "satisfied"
The organisers of last night's rally say that 200,000
citizens last night showed they wanted peaceful change...
▸▸

MORE FREE B92 DAILY NEWS

ANEM TV

VIDEO CLIP FROM
TODAYS RALLY IN
BELGRADE

Media
MEDIA REPRESSION IN
YUGOSLAVIA
WAR TIME DECREES
AND REGULATIONS
INTERVIEWS
STATEMENT
NEWS ON THE MEDIA
LINKS

Press

MEDIA REPRESSION

**HIGHER COMMERCIAL COURT DISMISSES B92
APPEAL**
BELGRADE, August 16 -- The Higher Commercial Court in
Belgrade has dismissed an appeal by former Radio B92
General Manager Sasa Mirkovic against a decision by the
Commercial Court appointing Aleksandar Nikacevic
general manager of the station...▸▸

Art&Society

NEW @ FREE B92

After 4 months off the air, Radio B2-92 resumed
broadcasting news and music on 99.1 FM, the third
frequency of Belgrade's Studio B Radio, on Monday
August 2 at 08.00 CET. The program is a continuation of
the real Radio B92 and its news and current affairs
programming is produced by the team that was evicted
from Radio B92 on April 2, when the station's
management was replaced by a government appointee.
The B2-92 program is on air daily from 08.00 - 20.00 CET
and provides national news coverage to audiences in
Belgrade, and throughout Serbia and Montenegro via the
ANEM radio and television networks. Real Audio and MP3
netcast will be available soon.

     PROGRAM
SCHEDULE

Multimedia
✚ Net Aid

FREEDOM OF
SPEECH FOR YOUR
SCREEN

Latuff - a brazilian cartoonist got
inspired by the Free B92 story. His
cartoons have ended as our favourite
desk top wallpapers.

Info Links
NEWS AGENCY BETA
(BELGRADE)
MONTENA-FAX
(PODGORICA)
WEEKLY MONITOR
(PODGORICA)
THE GUARDIAN
THE NEW YORK TIMES
ONEWORLD
INSTITUTE FOR WAR
AND PEACE REPORTING
GLOBALBEAT
STRATFOR
TRANSITIONAL
FOUNDATION FOR
PEACE AND FUTURE
RESEARCH
FREE SERBIA
ALTERNATIVE
INFORMATION
NETWORK IN THE
FORMER YUGOSLAVIA
MEDIA CLUB
(MONTENEGRO)
MEDIA CENTER
(BELGRADE)

Help&Support
SOLIDARITY FUND
SOLIDARITY ACTIONS
MESSAGES
CONTACT US

© Free B92, 1999

FIGURE 4.3   B92 homepage <http://b92eng.opennet.org/> in 1998

get bad media coverage and the endangered media get international support from colleagues around the world. Still, there seems to be a rather long learning curve for politicians to grasp that even seemingly 'local' media cannot, in a globalized information infrastructure, be censored at a national level for longer periods.

When the NATO air war against Serbia started in early 1999, media censorship became very strict. B92 was shut down again, mirrored on the WWW again, continued on, and reappeared again as B2-92 on a new frequency in mid-1999. With the increasing access to and use of the Internet and WWW, 'alternative' media may be coming into their own as parallel media. An example of this is the US-based radical journals such as *Mother Jones* and *CounterPunch*. In the midst of the NATO bombing campaign, they could distribute critical accounts of the air war. The other news was coming through.[34]

Establishing the South–South Link: Emailing the Third World

Finding ways of countering the informational and communications dominance of the North is a major concern for several groups of communications activists. One concern here is that the use of ICT, even for emancipatory purposes, may be replicating the electronic colonialization of the South by the North. This is not only in the sense of 'info-dumping' and the more obvious penetration by WWW broadcasting, but even in the very nature of the technology. Internet and WWW technologies are for the most part Northern, and perhaps even North American. One consequence of the commercialization of the Internet is that it is the rich end of the market that is the most interesting – no one wants to finance a T1 cable to an Indian village.[35] The danger here, as elsewhere in the globalized world economy, is that a large portion of the North and a narrow elite in the South breaks off, technologically speaking, from the rest of the world. Some attempts at maintaining a link into global networking will now be presented.

What does 'maintaining a link' mean? Concretely it means finding, applying and developing the communications tools for individuals and groups in the South to be part of the global communications infrastructure at a cost affordable even to those outside the elite. It also means getting these tools into the hands of people who can use

SANG⊕NeT

sn.apc.org

Southern Africa's Nonprofit Internet Service Provider

Member of the Association for Progressive Communications (APC)

Click the topic of your choice.

SANGONeT is a regional electronic information and communications network for development and human rights workers.

SANGONeT

- delivers **relevant information** to people working in development.
- has an **integrated approach** to communication and information networking.
- aims to **build capacity** in organisations through the use of electronic communication and information access.

" UKWABELANA NGOLWAZI NOMPHAKATHI "

NEWS | EDUCATION | OPEN GOVERNMENT | ENVIRONMENT LABOUR & ECONOMY | WOMEN | INFORMATION & TECHNOLOGY DEVELOPMENT | HEALTH | HOUSING | CULTURE | HUMAN RIGHTS

Have you found the SANGONeT site useful? Have you got any suggestions? We welcome your comments and suggestions.
websupport@sn.apc.org

FIGURE 4.4 SANGONeT homepage <http://www.sn.apc.org>

them. One such attempt at this was the *Marimba* project. This was an international collaborative effort to produce a communications software package that could be used on the simplest of computers, with low-speed modems over bad phone lines – something especially suited to voluntary associations working in the South. With financing from the Canadian International Development Research Centre (IDRC), the project was coordinated by the NirvCentre, provider of the Web electronic host service in Toronto (<www.web.apc.org>). Using the distributed team approach of communications hackerism, the Marimba team was spread out over North and South, Europe, Africa and Australia.

The Marimba package, when completed in the early 1990s, was intended both for the single user and for running a small host system off a simple DOS computer. Marimba includes both email and conferencing, based on the philosophy of open access in the sense discussed above: low cost and user friendliness. The package was composed of freeware components developed by communications hackers and made available for non-commercial purposes. Since this was before the widespread adoption of a TCP/IP standard and distribution of applications based on these standards, the basic package included components for FidoNet connectivity as well as for UUCP (UNIX-to-UNIX Copy Program). This enables a user to adapt to the type of host system he or she is connecting to. 'User friendliness' is, of course, somewhat subjective. This author was surprised to see that it only took about twenty minutes for a work-shop of women from all over South Asia to learn to send their first email ever using the Marimba package. A similar package called Windmail, built around the popular Pegasus Mail program, was built by people at the Dutch host Antenna.

Putting together and using such communications and small host packages was not enough, however. The small hosts, be they in Africa, Asia or Soviet eastern Europe had to have somewhere to connect to. The commercial and academic networks, running on UNIX machines and leased lines, were not open. Not until a door was hacked open. This door was dubbed a 'Fidogate', later using UUCP technology as well on a 'store and forward' basis. Through it, a small host system running FidoNet or UNIX software can gateway in to the Internet. The UK-based GreenNet, and several other APC member networks, pioneered this service. GreenNet alone was, at the end of 1997, gatewaying some thirty small hosts, in Africa, Asia, Europe, the Middle East and the Maghreb. Even as more and more small host systems start using Linux as a software base, they still often need somewhere to link up to. More important than this is the community of purpose and network of support that is developed in providing an information and communications infrastructure for voluntary associations and social movements.[36]

The work described above has expanded to a broader project called CABECA: Capacity Building for Electronic Communication in Africa. The goal of this IDRC-financed project is to promote computer networking throughout Africa, executed by the Pan African Development Information System (PADIS) of the United Nations Economic Commission for Africa (UNECA).

> While the rest of the world is traveling the global information super-highway of interconnected computer networks, which put a tremendous range of information facilities and services within reach of the general user, Africa stands the furthest removed of all the major regions of the world from the Information Age. At a time when the use of electronic communication to exchange information, transfer files and access data-bases is an everyday matter in many parts of the world, these techniques are still relatively unknown in Africa. Throughout the region, researchers, development professionals, business persons and others face severe difficulties in communicating among themselves and with their colleagues outside the region. Working in isolation, their work suffers from lack of information and duplication of efforts in a period of rapid socio-economic, technological and cultural change.[37]

Like other members in the APC community of networks, Green-Net operates with an eye to serving those people with email as their only access to electronic networking. Therefore, the development and use of software tools such as Majordomo and Listserv are given priority. These applications on a host server allow email users not only to subscribe to mailinglists, receiving electronic newsletters in their mailbox, but also to participate in an electronic forum. In other words, it is possible to participate in a many-to-many form of discussion using only email. Techniques are not enough, however. Knowledge on the use of such systems must also be distributed. So an integral part of the projects and programs carried out by the communication activists described here is training and sharing of experiences. The South Links project of the United Nations

Volunteers functioned in the same manner, providing a communications infrastructure between voluntary associations in the South.[38]

With the explosion of the WWW, many websites have appeared for organizing other websites and Internet resources. These guides, readily available for those with WWW access, become the defining instruments for what is 'sustainable development', 'children's rights', 'climate control', and so on. An example of such a site is the one maintained by the International Institute for Sustainable Development (<http://iisd1.iisd.ca/>). Information is put into a hierarchy and the agenda set through the selection presented. While well intended, the info-overload of the North overshadows any possible counter-agenda presentation by movements in the South.

When I am out presenting the material in this book, one question always arises. This is about the spread of progressive computing in the South. The line of thinking is this: if it is true that computer support for social action is available, and social action is sorely needed to improve the situation for the majority of the people on the planet, then it seems reasonable to assume that social movements in the South would go for this. This is of course happening. But the extent is unknown and probably unknowable. While progressive networks such as the APC community of networks, funding agencies, inter-state bodies and others are trying to provide support, there are many drawbacks. These have been treated under the section 'Barriers to Access' above, and 'Hurdles' below. It should be added that there is a more subtle barrier. This is the wariness of being dominated by support, with knowledge being a tool of control. There are some attempts to get around this.

The 'SouthLinks' project launched by the United Nations Volunteers was one attempt at strengthening South–South networking. Another is the work of the Third World Network, based in Malaysia. This is an independent non-profit international network of organizations and individuals involved in issues relating to development, the Third World and North–South issues. While the TWN and its related organizations have a broader agenda than computer-mediated communication and the WWW, these are important areas both for action and as means of countering Northern domination. One expression of this is 'The Peoples' Communication Charter' that restates the case for a New World Information and Communication Order (see Webography).

Providing Basic Public Service: The Blood Bank Network in South India

FOOD – Foundation of Occupational Development – is a Tamil Nadu NGO that channels government money into projects and programmes that the government in India cannot do, or has a track record of doing poorly. Examples of the work done are low-cost housing, self-employment schemes, local development planning for social services, rural health education, toilets for rural schools, and so on. FOOD retains a small percentage of the funding to finance itself. This type of implementation for development and social service projects has been found more cost-efficient than working through the public-sector bureaucracies. FOOD has several regional offices around the state of Tamil Nadu and acts as a consultant for projects in Sri Lanka and Mongolia.

As a member of Approtech Asia, FOOD set up in 1992/93 a FidoNet link to a system in the Philippines. This was not easy, given the state of Indian telephone lines and exchanges. Just getting a direct-dial international line could sometimes be something of an organizational accomplishment. Although the Indian Institutes of Technology were producing large numbers of qualified computer technicians and programmers, the majority of these went down the brain drain to the USA and it was hard to find people willing to spend time and money on electronic networking for social service. After years of experimenting with various software alternatives and BBS systems, they have settled in to a dial-up Linux-based host system. Their BBS system is called EasyLink, their web address is <www.xlweb.com>. Since the telecom sector in general and the Internet sector in particular have until recently been the preserve of state monopolies, getting and maintaining Internet connectivity at a cost affordable for an NGO has been a major task. Regulations covering Internet service providers have started to relax in India so access should increase.

The EasyLink BBS system in Chennai (Madras) had in mid-1997 about a thousand users, with about four hundred NGOs online. They use differential pricing so that commercial/private users subsidize NGO and student users. One very interesting use is that they are organizing communications between bloodbanks in a Blood Bank Network Operation. This grew out of the meeting of experience in two fields: developmental and social work concerning health educational and service provision, and computer mediated communications. There has been a shortage of blood in the state of Tamil Nadu, so programs to enable what is available to be used efficiently and to increase the supply of high-quality blood for hospitals have been given high priority. The online Blood Bank Network maintains a database of blood available, allowing exchanges to take place between government, private and NGO bloodbanks. In addition, educational material and medical information is spread, for example concerning testing, AIDS, and so on.

Maintaining a reliable host system has been a challenge in the face of poor telephone connections and power failures. So one planned extension of the EasyLink system is for wireless modems across the state of Tamilnadu and neighbouring Kerala, connecting FOOD offices and five sub-hosts already polling in to EasyLink. This is an example of how an NGO is using computer-mediated communications to provide a basic, necessary social service. The blood-bank system has been replicated by FOOD in Colombo, Sri Lanka. This use of ICT for supporting logistics in developmental situations is gaining ground, with reports and evaluations of such uses appearing in ever greater number. One example is the collection of examples found in the booklet *networking for development* by Paul Starkey. In focus here are two networks in Africa working on issues of animal traction as support for developing agriculture.[39]

Democratizing Knowledge: The GK97

One of the potentials of the Internet and World Wide Web is for the dissemination of knowledge. Whether the new technology will indeed be used for spreading knowledge is still an open question. There is the very real danger that this possibility in the new technology to inform and educate will, like radio and television before, fall prey to commercialized infantilization or worse. What knowledge is, and what education and learning comprise, are perennial topics of dispute. When information and communication technology is applied in this area, ideological choices become mandatory and ideological stances manifest. One has to choose between a broadcasting paradigm and the communications paradigm as the dominant mode of information.

While scholars have for some time been both talking about distributed knowledge systems and putting this into practice in various ways for research, communication activists are now starting to realize this potential. A systematic example of this is the GK97 – the Knowledge for Development/Global Knowledge Conference held in 1997. The major focus of this physical and virtual conference was on development. It was organized by the Canadian Web Community of Networks, with financing from the Canadian International Development Authority (CIDA) and the International Development Research Centre (IDRC). Organized as a global think-tank around the questions of what 'knowledge for development' might mean and be, and of the role of ICT in development and its impact on the South and North–South and South–South relations. A special focus was on women and the new technology.

Using a methodology tested at a series of United Nations summits since Rio in 1992, the physical and virtual conferences meshed and complemented each other. Input came from those not there and news went out rapidly and directly to participants around the world. Technically, this was organized into several online multilingual conferences:

a.Gender (gk97.gender) Conference. Using a recent report on Gender and Information Technology, prepared by the APC Women's Programme, this list focuses on some of the most important practical considerations facing women and women's organizations around the world. The gk97.gender list will be open from now until the end of September. Suggestions and strategies culled from these discussions will be prepared for presentation at the GK97 physical conference.

b.Storyline (gk97.storyline) Conference (Starts May 13) This list exists to ask the question: What is Knowledge for Development? The Storyline is intended to be a jumping-off point, outlining the key challenges of the information age, and their relevance for communities in developing countries. Your contribution to this list (whether optimistic or skeptical, theoretical or experience-based) will directly feed into the conference in Toronto.

c.Information Technology and Development: Lessons Learned (gk97. lessons) Conference (Starts May 20) Set the record straight! The focus of this list will be the experiences of APC users and others who have triumphed, struggled or been by-passed during the information revolution. This list invites you to share examples of best practices, and to develop ideas, strategies and projects that challenge, take advantage of and/or subvert the current information mania. Drawing directly upon these discussions, a formal presentation will be made to the GK97 physical conference in Toronto.

These conferences were available through email for those electronic communicators unable to access a hostserver carrying the conferences in newsgroup formats. Proceedings and other materials were also available at WWW sitings. One was the CIDA Village Well Gathering Site at <http://www.villagewell.gk97.gc.ca> that branched out into a forum for school participation on education and development issues. An important aspect of the GK97 experience is that it showed a large degree of reflexivity – that is, that *emancipatory electronic networking was beginning to reflect back upon itself and to define itself as an independent element in the process of social change.*

There are other examples of the use of ICT for democratizing knowledge. As Michael Polman and Peter van der Pouw Kraan point out in their book *Van Bolwerken tot Netwerken* (From Bulwarks to Networks), distributed knowledge systems such as the HIVNET BBS, started in Amsterdam in 1990, have meant much for the dissemination of medical knowledge about HIV and AIDS. This has been important both as support for those afflicted and in the work of prevention.[40] Those interested in homeopathic medicine were early users of CMC, establishing global electronic networks in the 1980s.

The documentation gathered in and around the GK97 shows that the WWW is developing as a distributed knowledge system for social change. The social epistemology of the Net is important here, since it defines which knowledge will be distributed and which knowledge will be withheld. The GK97 also shows signs of an emerging distributed cognition system regarding knowledge and social change.

Advocacy, Campaigning, Insurgency and the Electronic Fabric of Struggle

Information and communication technology, the Internet and the World Wide Web can be put to the use of furthering an emancipatory cause. Amnesty International is an organization that uses ICT to strengthen its work. Amnesty is built on a decentralized basis, with local 'cells' adopting a political prisoner or prisoners. The local group then pressures authorities, publicizes the case of each prisoner of conscience, and basically never gives up. National and international chapters of Amnesty, having pooled resources and having developed a quite effective fundraising apparatus, are able to field a number of researchers who do high-quality watchdogging on human rights issues. The annual Amnesty report on various regions and countries receives wide publicity and is used as source material for programmes and intergovernmental policies. In an organization that is both local and global and that relies on making transgressions of human rights known, ICT is a big asset. Internal materials are circulated quickly, governments pressured, press releases distributed and documentation made widely available thanks to ICT.

The new technology can also be used for a more focused, single-issue type of campaigning. An example of this was the campaign against the launching of NAFTA, the North American Free Trade Association. In his study of this movement campaign, Howard Frederick writes that NGO computer networking against the US–Canada Free Trade Agreement (FTA) began in 1987. Beginning in Canada, organizations there and in the USA and Mexico began joining together in their opposition to what was seen as an arrangement one-sidedly in favour of capital. Besides the usual campaigning tools of lobbying, petitioning and public opinion-making, the anti-NAFTA coalition started using computer networking. A new breed of 'keyboard warriors' emerged in organizations such as the Minneapolis-based Institute for Agriculture and Trade Policy (IATP), the Mexican NGO Red Mexican de Acción Frente al Libre Comercio (RMALC). Many other organizations of farmers, peasants, environmentalists, workers and women joined in the online anti-NAFTA coalition.[41] However, the 'fast-track' strategy of the US government succeeded in passing the NAFTA draft agreement before the opposition could muster. One spin-off, however, was the growth of NGO computer networking in Mexico. Interest in using the new technology for social purposes eventually resulted in the establishment of the LaNeta network.

On the day the NAFTA took effect in 1994, the liberation movement EZLN, better known as the Zapatistas, rose in armed rebellion in the jungles of the Chiapas in southern Mexico. In a seminal article 'The Zapatistas and the Electronic Fabric of Struggle', Harry Cleaver writes:

In the narrow terms of traditional military conflict, the Zapatista uprising has been confined to a limited zone in Chiapas. However, through their ability to extend their political reach via modern computer networks, the Zapatistas have woven a new electronic fabric of struggle to carry their revolution throughout Mexico and around the world.

... a key aspect of the state's war against the Zapatistas (both in Mexico and elsewhere) has been its ongoing efforts to isolate them, so that they can be destroyed or forced to accept co-optation. In turn, the Zapatistas and their supporters have fought to maintain and elaborate their political connections throughout the world. This has been a war of words, images, imagination and organization in which the Zapatistas have had surprising success.[42]

Vital to this continuing struggle is the use of computer-mediated communication. Harry Cleaver points out that, despite a lot of media hype when it was discovered that poor people in a rural corner of Mexico were venturing out into cyberspace, Subcommandante Marcos is not sitting in a jungle camp keyboarding out his communiqués via a mobile telephone and computer on to the Internet. Instead, messages are smuggled through the lines and then transmitted. However, there were some reports that the February 1996 ceasefire eventually arrived at was negotiated in some way via computer-mediated communication (*Time* picked up on this, *inter alia*). When the struggle is carried out into the new electronic media, it is easier to mobilize a web of solidarity and to keep in contact with this network of support. As in other electronic campaigns, the necessary components are here: linkages of a support network of individuals and organizations (email), facilities for information exchange and coordination of activities (electronic conferences such as <indig.info>and <reg.mexico>), channels for broadcasting, and an archive with historical material, Chiapas 95, found at the University of Texas, and an electronic book, *Zapatistas! Documents of the New Mexican Revolution*.[43]

The result of such processes interweaving cyberspace and other zones of human space is a new composition of social relationships increasingly difficult for capitalists and the state to manage. Precisely to the degree that its self-elaboration has been outstripping the ability of managers of capitalist society to repress or co-opt, this growing 'social' composition has moved beyond a 'class' composition. It is not merely the self-reconfigured structure of power by workers against their exploiters; with new threads and new weaves, the social fabric is being rewoven into textures with less and less of a 'class' character. This self-activity, of course, continues to be constrained by the oppression of classes, but it increasingly weaves according to its own innovative designs.[44]

Despite attempts by governments to curb the effects of 'cross-border coalitions' using electronic networking through repression, restrictive legislation, co-optation and other means, Cleaver is optimistic about the inherent possibilities of global electronic networking in creating an alternative without a central command post or hierarchy. While Harry Cleaver saw the Zapatistas and Chiapas movement have some democratizing impact on the political system in Mexico, this does not seem to be leading to a stable peace agreement between the government and the insurgents.[45]

From He-male to (Sh)email: Creating a Gender-Sensitive Technology

An obvious feature of ICT is that it is 'pale and male'. Because of its history and origins, computing, even in its hackerish forms, has been mainly a domain for white males. However, the type of 'flat' networking made possible using computer-mediated communication should, according to the literature, be more accommodating to the style of organizing found among women. So it is not surprising that women's networks have been developing that either use or focus on computer networking. There are many examples here of implementations, projects, programmes that are not only using ICT but are also trying to develop new tools for making the technology more gender-sensitive.

The UN Conference on Women held in Beijing in 1995 was something of a surfacing for ICT as a means for furthering women's rights. The groundwork had been started long before, for example in the Women's Project run by a team from several APC member and partner networks. One result of this was that the APC fielded an all-women team of technicians and communication activists that took care of NGO information and communication flows before, during and after the Beijing Conference. A number of key documents on women and information technology were produced. Since these documents are maintained and continuously spread through electronic communications, the positions agreed upon by the governments will not 'go away' but are used as organizing tools by organizations and social movements. The Independent Committee on Women and Global Knowledge is one such watchdog organization, active in the issue area of women and information technology. Their position is summed up in the following:

> We agree that there are at least three basic principles essential to ensuring sound planning for ICT development and design:
> 1. designs of ICT systems that ensure that men and women have equal opportunity to be involved in every facet of ICT development, from infrastructure through to front-end use, recognizing that this may involve strategies to support the contributions of and address the barriers to women's full participation;
> 2. assessments of the differential impacts on both men and women of the effects of any and all ICT development programmes;
> 3. evaluations of ICT development to take into account the distinct situations and resources of women and men, to ensure that all have continuous learning.
>
> None of this is possible without the concerted effort of all development sectors to support women's full participation in decision making, access to, contributions to and benefits from the generation of knowledge for development.
>
> THREE CRITICAL PRIORITY ACTIONS
>
> Policy and decision makers, investors, civil society organizations and donor agencies are encouraged, therefore, to:
> 1. incorporate gender analysis in all scientific and technological policy research;
> 2. develop and finance follow-up and evaluation mechanisms to identify and measure the impact of ICT initiatives on women's communications needs;
> 3. work in partnership with women and the organizations that they represent in all aspects and at all levels of technical training and education, access and delivery systems, and in the development of information systems specific to the needs of women.[46]

There are numerous women's nets and websites with a presence on the WWW. The example presented here is 'brown and female': the South Asian Women's NETwork, SAWNET. This is a 'linking website' that puts together both links to other sources of information and is itself a repository of information at a high level of intellectual, cultural and political sophistication. While bearing the unmistakable stamp of diasporic Indians – lots of material on the movies – it is the manifestation of a cross-border coalition made possible through the use of ICT. And the borders crossed are not necessarily friendly: India, Pakistan, Bangladesh, Sri Lanka, Nepal, Burma, and Bhutan. While the SAWNET website is a product of academia, it shows the social concerns of intellectual women from South Asia. The linkages to NGOs presented on SAWNET may be leading to closer links between intellectuals, both non-resident and resident, and grassroots NGOs. Since south Indian social movements is a field of teaching and research for me, I have had a special interest in monitoring this process and see developments in this direction. Also, a careful and thorough Internet search of websites pertaining to South Asia in general and India in particular shows that there is no 'male' South Asian site comparable to SAWNET. 'Comparable' here means in terms of social direction and cultural content. One interpretation of this is that women are marking out a new social trail in cyberspace.

It is both common and research knowledge that women have less of a chance than men in having their voice heard in the 'public sphere'. This is because the sphere of public activity of politics, business and organizations has been shaped by and for men. The power of the word is the power to dictate social contracts: for example, the gender contract – the underlying dynamics of gender relations that are taken for granted. A question being asked increasingly in the literature on CMC is how the new technology reshapes writing, communication patterns and possibly forms of thought. A related question is whether the possibilities of ICT may be providing a support for renegotiating the gender contract.

In a companion volume to this book, *women@internet*, Wendy Harcourt has collected and commented on a collection of experiences made by activists/scholars in the attempt at the construction of a cyberculture for women. The questions asked are whether the new information and communication technology can empower women in their quest for equality, and, more specifically, if the new technology offers the freedom to create something new in the realm of gender relationships. There are a number of experiences and arguments that suggest that this may be so. Computer-mediated communication can break the nature of 'place' and hence break the link between gender and place: the female *body* as the defining characteristic of the role of women, the domestic *place* of the home as a delimiting domain for

FIGURE 4.5   SAWNET homepage <http://www.umiacs.umd.edu/users/sawweb/sawnet/>

women and in the hitherto male-dominated public *sphere* that regulates women to subordinate roles.[47]

The experiences related in the book, based in part on building an online community, points, once again, to the fact that online groups can break out of virtuality into self-awareness of being something more than a mailing list; that 'cyberorgs' can open up a field for social experimentation; and in this, create something new. If nothing else, it offers new metaphors for how we can think about human interaction. In this author's view and experience, it is not a mere coincidence that these aspects of unfolding new dimensions in the application of ICT – of stretching the 'better' into the 'beyond' – are appearing where women are most. The concrete examples of experiments can be found in the numerous 'women's nets' appearing on the World Wide Web (see Figure 4.5 and the Webography).

Notes

1. I tried this on 9 December 1997 using AltaVista search engine and got 36,730,493 returns for the WWW and 5,548,458 for UseNet.
2. See Ben H. Bagdikian, *The Media Monopoly*, 4th edn, Boston 1992.
3. Alex Carey, *Taking The Risk Out of Democracy: Corporate Propaganda versus Freedom and Liberty*, Illinois 1997 (reprint).
4. Edward S. Herman and Noam Chomsky, *Manufacturing Consent: The Political Economy of the Mass Media*, New York 1988.
5. Republished in shorter version in *OM (Ordfront Magasin)*, May 1997.
6. Charles Scheiner, PO Box 1182, White Plains, New York 10602 USA; telephone: 1 914 428 7299; fax: 1 914 428 7383; Internet: <cscheiner @igc.apc.org>. For information on East Timor, write <timor-info@igc. apc.org>. Charles Scheiner is National Coordinator, East Timor Action Network/US Internet: <etan-us@igc.apc.org>.
7. Tiger Li, 'Computer-Mediated Communications and the Chinese Students in the U.S.', *Information Society*, vol. 7, 1990, p. 129.
8. Ibid., p. 133.
9. Ibid., pp. 133–4.
10. Ibid., p. 134.
11. Ibid., p. 135.
12. Noam Chomsky has authored numerous books and articles on this topic. APC networks carry a special 'Chomsky conference', collecting otherwise unpublished speeches and interviews since 1991, called <chomsky.views>
13. Tim Sharp, 'West Papua: The "Other" Timor', in <reg.westpapua>, 1996–11–14 on APC systems.

14. Carmel Budiardjo and Liem Soei Liong, 'West Papua: The Obliteration of a People' *TAPOL*, 3rd edn, 1988, p. 25. Quoted by Tim Sharp, 'West Papua'.
15. Tim Sharp, 'West Papua'.
16. <reg.westpapua> 24 November 1996.
17. An examination of the state of electronic organizing shows the following (19 November 1997): 'OPMRC'= eight hits, six referring back to TWICS; others were cross-references.
18. At <http://www.cs.utexas.edu/users/cline/papua/core.htm>.
19. Mark Doris, 'WEST PAPUA: THE CASE FOR RE-EXAMINATION', in <reg.westpapua> on APC Action, and is reached at <wpaireland @gn.apc.org>.
20. Mika Böök, 'SOVIET COUP on-line at the front-line', *Interdoc Europe Newsletter*, no. 5, October 1991, p. 8; cf. 'The World is Wired', *San Francisco Bay Guardian*, 11 September 1991.
21. Böök, 'SOVIET COUP'.
22. The definition intended here is that of Karl Popper in his classic *The Open Society and its Enemies*, London 1966.
23. At <http://www.soros.org/burma.html>.
24. <reg.burma> Topic 6754 Burma and Network connection, 26 May 1997 (at macpsy.ucsf.EDU). From: tun@macpsy.ucsf.EDU (Coban Tun).
25. Swedish Radio, P1, *Lunch Eko*, 10 October 1997.
26. *Dagens nyheter*, 11 October 1997.
27. <http://www.npaid.no>.
28. 'Chronology of the Movement to Ban Landmines as of 14th October 1997', at <http://www.npaid.no>.
29. The writings of historian Timothy Garton Ash are especially illuminating in this regard.
30. From the official homepage of Protest '96: <http://galeb.etf.bg.ac.yu/~protest96/>
31. <yugo.antiwar> 9/19/96 Topic 4191 Promocija Odraz B92 vesti beograd @cogent.net.
32. <yugo.antiwar> 9/04/95 Topic 3656 Croatia: Indep. Radio loses licence, M.JUNG@GAIA.comlink.apc.org.
33. Sveriges Radio, P1, Luncheko, 29 November 1996.
34. Bob Harris, 'Kosovo – Fighting the War Crimes', 25 May 1999, at <http://www.motherjones.com/scoop>. *CounterPunch* kept a careful monitor of the NATO campaign. This coverage is archived at <http://www.counterpunch.org/serbia.html>.
35. See this author's 'The Telecom Policy Process in India', presented at South Asian Scholar's Conference, Madison, Wisconsin, October 1997.
36. The GreenNet homepages cover this work.<http://www.gn.apc.org>. Pegasus Networks in Australia services small hosts in the Asia–Pacific rim. <http://www.peg.apc.org>.

37. <http://www.gn.apc.org>.
38. <http://www.unv.org>.
39. Paul Starkey, *networking for development*, published by the International Forum for Rural Transport and Development, London 1997. See also <http://www.gn.apc.org/ifrtd>. Information on FOOD work presented directly to this author, who has functioned as an unpaid CMC consultant to FOOD since 1993.
40. Michael Polman and Peter van der Pouw Kraan, *Van Bolwerken tot Netwerken*, Amsterdam 1995, ch. 9.
41. Howard H. Frederick, 'Computer Communications in Cross-Border Coalition-Building: North American NGO Networking Against NAFTA', *Gazeta*, no. 50, 1992, p. 217–41.
42. This quote and following from Harry Cleaver, 'The Zapatistas and the Electronic Fabric of Struggle', at <http://www.eco.utexas.edu/Homepages/Faculty/Cleaver/>.
43. The Zapatista book can be found at <gopher://lanic.utexas.edu:70/11/la/Mexico/Zapatistas; and a pamphlet can be found at <http://www.physics.mcgill.ca/WWW/oscarh/RSM/neng-pamph.html>. The archive is found at <gopher://eco.utexas.edu/mailinglists/Chiapas95> or <http://www.eco.utexas.edu:80/Homepages/Faculty/Cleaver/chiapas95.html>.
44. See note 42.
45. Peter Gellert, 'Mexican government rejects Chiapas peace proposal', January 1997, at <http://www.peg.apc.org/~stan/260/260p16c.htm>.
46. Found at <http://www.postindustrial.com/morewomen/canon. html>, 19 June 1997.
47. Wendy Harcourt (ed.), *Women@internet*, London 1999. For discussion of 'place' see especially the chapter by Arturo Escobar, 'Gender, Place and Networks: A Political Ecology of Cyberculture', pp. 31–54.

5

Computer Support for Emancipatory Action

The 'winnowing and shifting' of examples of computer support for social action presented in the preceding chapters have resulted in the generation of twelve different categories. This has been done using some of the basic tools of qualitative analysis. Each category has enough internal coherence and boundary demarcation to be considered a type. These are:

- *Media substitution*   Standard broadcast media can be circumvented. Information can be de-mediated.
- *Creating interaction*   Individuals and groups can find each other.
- *Enhancing interaction:* offline groups and organizations can intensify their interactions.
- *Breaking the censorship of silence.*
- *Electronic perforation*   Closed societies can be opened up.
- *Bypassing hierarchy*   Electronic communication tends to flatten hierarchies.
- *Crisis communications*   Computer-mediated communication is robust under duress.
- *Linking the periphery*   South-bound information flows can be supported.
- *Public service and developmental intervention*   Logistical and communications support.
- *Distributing knowledge*   Experiences from work in social change are shared and built upon.
- *Advocacy*   Individuals and groups can organize and campaign for their cause.
- *Renegotiation of social contracts*   The dynamism of technology can be a vehicle for restructuring human relationships, for example the gender contract.

It is hoped that this typology of computer support for social action will aid in the understanding of one direction of use for information and communication technology. It is also hoped that this list will be challenged through augmentation – that is, in continued experimentation in the search for new and meaningful ways to use the new technology.

Politics is not just substance, it is also symbolism. Much of what we call politics is symbolic action.[1] The purpose of symbolic acts is to increase the legitimacy of those performing them through the appellation to, and creation of, a broader consensual meaning. Communication and information exchanges in the sense brought out in this book can be viewed as a form of symbolic political action. The very act of connecting to other like-minded people on the other side of the globe to bring about social change is in itself of symbolic, and political, importance. It increases not only effectiveness, releasing the synergy of interaction, but also the legitimacy of those involved.

Ideas on an expanding public sphere as a social place for communicative exchange provide a starting point for understanding the meaning of citizens' networks and their support for social action.[2] One insight is that continued commodification of information might increase alienation toward the new technology. Another is that the application of information technology as communicative praxis may strengthen civil society and the autonomy of individuals. Concretely, this means that computer-mediated communication provides a new forum, on a global basis, for a wide participation in a public dialogue and critical discourse. Among those involved in constructing CMC systems there is a consciousness and a purposefulness in the work of creating not just one new forum but a whole array of *agorae*.[3]

The Communications Activists: The Salt of Cyberspace

The communications activists – as individuals, teams and a community – are a many-faceted set. At least five different dimensions have been uncovered. These are the communications hackers, the netweavers, the networkers, the supporters, and the observers.

The communications hackers The communications hackers are the 'techies' who gather and produce the tools for low-cost computer-mediated communications and develop applications suitable for social computing. These are the people who developed the FidoNet set of software communication tools, who built the gateways between small host systems and the Internet, who are applying Linux in faraway places and producing other low-cost, free packages.

The netweavers The netweavers are those who interconnect info-workers and media tighter into modes of co-operation and inter-action. The netweavers are not themselves information technology network builders, but deal with the coordination of network builders, offering both a practical and ideological forum for the discussion of information technology and social movements. Examples here are the Union for Democratic Communications (UDC), InterDoc and the Third World Network.

The UDC is one of many groups worried about the course that information technology may be taking. Their by-line is: 'Communications should be about people, not money. The UDC is a group of activists and academics who promote people-based, not-so-corporate ways of talking to each other.'[4] Their viewpoints are distributed in their multilingual *The Democratic Communiqué*.

InterDoc started as an international partnership of NGOs and NGO networks using information for social change. InterDoc represents an attempt at self-organization within civil society: a long-term project both to understand the possibilities and dangers of information technology and computer-mediated communication and to reduce duplication of effort and promote a sharing of resources.[5] This model of drawing together NGOs from a certain interest area into an 'umbrella network' to coordinate the collection and distribution of information is appearing elsewhere. An example of this is HURIDOCS (Human Rights Documentation).

The networkers The networkers are those engaged in the concrete organizational work of providing an information and communication infrastructure for social movements and voluntary associations. Several networks cater to such organizations. These networks have not coalesced under a single organizational umbrella, even though the standardization of the Internet protocols and WWW tools facilitate inter-exchanges on the technical level.

The supporters Groups and organizations working within, and for, 'civil society' are chronically underfunded. Investing in information technology and setting up systems for computer-mediated communication can be expensive. Fortunately, several favourable foundations have financially supported different attempts at creating an informational infrastructure for groups in civil society. For example, the MacArthur Foundation in the USA has helped the Institute for Global Communications (PeaceNet, EcoNet, etc.). In Sweden, such support went through the state, and NordNet there has received grants from a special funding programme for support to peace initiatives. Nicarao in Managua has received support from the Norwegian development aid agency. In Britain, Church bodies have been supportive of increasing use of computer-mediated communication for social, human rights and developmental purposes. Also in Britain, there has been support from the labour movement and from the city council of Manchester in setting up the Manchester Host. Another type of non-financial support is that provided by organizations such as the Electronic Frontier Foundation (EFF).

The observers   One type of observer to the phenomenon of computer-mediated communication in civil society is a few academics. Some have backgrounds in communications and media, some are technicians who begin discussing the social consequences of the new information technology. This author obviously belongs in this category, with the observation that working on this subject matter is like being a contemporary archeologist: small fragments are strewn around in the instant debris of information society. The task is to put the pieces together into a larger pattern. Here coincidence and wishful thinking are always two dangers. Here is an example: in this book, I argue that there is something that can be called 'computer lib' and that the appearance, development and spread of an operating system such as Linux may be an important part of this. I also argue that the new type of social networking, with flat hierarchies and communication in focus, may be more female than male. So, with these glasses on my conceptual eyes, I 'discovered' that the *Linux Journal* is basically run by women and the *Windows Journal* by men.[6] Coincidence?

In eight years' work on this text, I have noticed my own tendency to start mixing 'communication' with 'communications'. The former denotes the act of communicating, related to a context, a sender and a recipient. The latter denotes the means for conveying the act and substance. This linguistic slide is, I hope, more than just a lapse in attention on my part. I am suggesting, again and in another way, that here is a question of theoretical importance: how and when does the means mesh with the message? This is a question of performance put in the first chapter. It is perhaps in the convergence of the two that change occurs.

The Impetus to Access

> The new global giants are doing more than expanding their control over the technological instruments that issue news, information, and entertainment. They and their subsidiaries are also gathering up world copyrights of earlier information and popular culture: archives of news, magazines, books, television programs, film libraries, and musical compositions. Much of what used to be free in libraries or inexpensive for the average consumer is rapidly growing in cost, thanks to exclusive corporate ownership. Examples include important statistics now in data banks available only for a fee or scholarly journals with greatly increased subscription costs.
>
> Ben H. Bagdikian, *The Media Monopoly*

Several factors increase the impetus to access of information and communication technologies, besides increasing effectiveness and legitimacy. One is the growing concern over the capitalistic monopolization of the production, storage and distribution of information. Another is censorship. Therefore access becomes a central democratic concern. The success of CNN (Cable News Network) shows that people are concerned about their electronic global village. The use of media like CNN by politicians and the military, for example in the 1991 Gulf War, also shows again that there is a need for media providing uncensored criticism.[7]

The electronic agora: discourse or noise?

Many observers of the WWW/Internet explosion in the 1990s have seen not the development of an electronic meeting place for considered discussion but a place for a cacophony of monologues. Not debate but noise. This is sometimes seen as an extension of an apparent fragmentation of media such as television and radio, with XXX number of channels appearing, each adding to the entropy of cultural meaning.[8] While the latter point is a strong observation,

The agora, a real world metaphor

In the centre of the city where I live, Stockholm, there is a square known as Hay Market Square. As the name suggests, this is an old place – it is a long time since horses got their hay here. It is a classic urban square – it is even geometrically square, paved in square granite cobble. The open square is now mainly used for numerous fruit and vegetable stands run by the gamut of immigrants. The discourse here is many-tongued. The north side of the square opens to one of the main streets in Stockholm, King's Street (Kungsgatan). The west side is flanked by a large department store, PUB. This is not a place for drink but is named after the founder, Paul Urban Byström. The store, now owned by the large cooperative movement, has a special claim to fame: V.I. Lenin, as an old ad runs, carried out the October Revolution in a suit from PUB. He stopped in Stockholm on his way to the Finland station in 1917 to visit a mistress and do some final research at the National Archives on the collapse of capitalism and imperialism.

The south side of Hay Market Square has a new glass menagerie, a multiplex cinema with adjacent fast-food place. This is right above the escalator down to the classic underground market for multi-ethnic food. The stalls and cafés in this culinary United Nations are usually crowded, and noisy. On the east side of the square is the impressive Concert Hall, fronted by stone stairs and a large Carl Miles sculpture of Apollo at his harp surrounded by the muses. The stairs are a favourite meeting place. Rendezvous are made or broken, ice-cream eaten, departures started or ended. But mostly people just come and sit and Do Nothing Useful.

When children Do Nothing Useful, we call it play. When grown-ups do it, we call it Wasting Time. There is, however, another way of looking at Doing Nothing Useful. It can also be seen as exercising the right of autonomy. So the analogy sought for here would be that while most of the space in the electronic agora will be occupied by global shopkeepers, many small and one large, there is also room for some culture, both popular and fine arts, and above all for countless passers-by who can Do What They Want and meet who they want. I am reminded that the first public protest in Sweden against the US war in Vietnam was held on this square in 1965. At the time, this was definitely Nothing Useful and demonstrators got their heads smashed by the police. But this single protest sparked one of the largest popular movements in Swedish history, mobilized and politically educated a generation of young Swedes, changed Swedish foreign policy, providing a haven for American war resisters, and probably made a long-term impact on Swedish political culture. All from Doing Nothing Useful in this public place.

there may be another way of looking at the 'chaos' of the WWW and Internet. This is beside the obvious consideration that an apparent fragmentation on the consumer side does not reflect the concentration on the owner side.

A first point would be that the new technology has not created the plurality of the world. It has, however, made some of the plurality visible by allowing individuals and groups who would otherwise be silent and invisible to be seen and heard. This is the *empowering* capability of the technology. A second point would be that 'chaos' is usually defined from within a modernistic paradigm. The 'modern' can be defined not only as the self-referring contemporary but also as secure centrality. The latter definition is the one presented by Stephen Toulmin in his book *Cosmopolis – The Hidden Agenda of Modernity*.[9] An important component of modernity is the drive for a rational 'centre' that can exercise control, overview, provide an agreed upon meaning, define the terms, provide a total ideology for the basis of scientific, rational society. But in another, non-hierarchical worldview, hierarchy gives out to networking, hegemony to autonomy.

Constructions

Information and communication technology seems to be fostering new (sub)cultures. In these subcultures, new norms develop and new patterns of behaviour emerge. Some of these norms can be described in the following way. Originally the Internet, both by definition and policy, embraced a non-commercial ethic. A self-regulating 'netiquette' emerged that is often offended by trying to sell products, or opinions, to people who did not ask for them. Known as 'spamming', this unsolicited email has aroused protests and calls for regulation. But commercials are being packaged into many a website and videoclip. And if you accept the commercials, free email is available.

Another example of the non-commercial ethic that has developed on the Net is that of keeping material free and programs 'public domain' or at least 'shareware'. This subculture is also outspokenly libertarian and instinctively allergic to government control. This was vividly illustrated by the reaction to a proposal by the US government, presented by vice-president Al Gore in February 1994, for a 'clipper chip'. This electronic encryption component would be installed in telephones and the key would be in the hands of US government surveillance authorities. The official motivation for this was crime prevention. The networking community saw the proposal as an infringement of free speech and freedom of (electronic) assembly. Hackers immediately started making and distributing their own encryption and code-breaking software, in effect putting the law enforcement agencies in a worse position than they were in before the clipper chip proposal was announced.[10]

What will fill the vacuum after the apparent collapse of ideology? This question is being voiced in many different ways. Will it be one global 'free' market, with globicops policing offenders? Or can it be something else? It has been suggested, and actively pursued, that NGOs can play an important role in filling the vacuum with meaningful human activity – meaningful in the sense of planetary survival – and that NGO use and organization of new electronic media such as computer-mediated communication is giving NGOs a comparative advantage that they have until now not had. Civil society has an important place in cyberspace.[11]

'Cyberspace' is a term increasingly used to denote the forward fringe of an emerging information society. The older usage of the root word in the term cybernetics, meaning the conscious self-correcting steering of large systems, is close to the Greek origin meaning helmsman. Cyberspace is conceived as a situation in which enormous amounts of information, indeed the whole of recorded human knowledge, is available to anyone, anytime, anywhere, in an interactive and communicative way. Obviously we have not arrived there yet, but more and more people – scientists, business people, politicians and social activists – are starting to think and talk about what this can imply. Actually, H.G. Wells started writing about a 'world brain' in the 1930s. But since this is experienced as new, thinking tends to be in terms of metaphors – extrapolations and comparisons with what is already known.

Some think of cyberspace in a *geographical metaphor*. Cyberspace is seen as a 'new frontier' to be colonized. These people think in terms of 'digital highways' and push for the construction of an informational infrastructure.[12] Some think in the *multi-media metaphor* with visions of expanding new markets. Some think in terms of an *informed citizens' metaphor*. What looms beyond the digital horizon is some kind of teledemocracy to recapture a dwindling political legitimacy. Some are thinking in the *meta-library metaphor*. The impetus here is to organize and structure both the information and the gatekeepers. These types of metaphoric thinking reflect, of course, various interests and perspectives of those thinking these thoughts.

In his innovative work *Gödel, Escher, Bach* Douglas Hofstadter has illustrated the dependency of the content of thought on the form of thought.[13] Putting new wine in old barrels may leave us with intellectual vinegar. In the situation of innovative chaos that faces the world at the end of the millennium, movements for social change are proposing a different, *experimental metaphor* for grasping the opportunities of cyberspace. It is one in which people are neither consumers nor citizens but ethically empowered individuals working in association, yet without spatial or hierarchical organization. In this social experimentation there are, of course, many hurdles.

Hurdles

One obstacle to optimum emancipatory computer-mediated communication is that the emerging systems tend to be 'pale and male'. In the nature of things – the existing world economic and political order – information technology started with and is still largely in the hands of the North. And within the North access to the technology is for those with the education to cross over the digital threshold, and money is still important. Even among progressive networkers and users of computer-mediated communication there is probably an overwhelming dominance of Caucasian males. The metaphoric 'global electronic village' is not a hamlet of utopian socialism. As in the heat and dust of the real villages of the world – where the overwhelming majority of humanity lives – there are the rich and poor, the outcasts on the fringe, the sharecroppers, the illiterate and the few in control of the crops and the stores.

Linked to this is another sociological factor: North Americanism. Since the USA is the leader in developing, and marketing, innovations in information technology, there is sometimes a spillover tendency to 'follow the leader' even in 'better' applications. This problem of 'California surfing' on the new wave of technology may lead to a gap between the 'grasstops', ever more adept in technological innovation, and the 'grassroots' applications. The innovation rate on the user side is always going to be much slower than the accelerating pace of innovation on the technical side. There is a danger of this tendency being enhanced through the external funding of NGO communications projects and systems.[14] A definite danger is that external funding sources – that is, outside the NGO community – can disrupt the agenda, perhaps even adding to information entropy and organizational fragmentation.

It has been suggested that the introduction of CMC into the work of NGOs in the South may have some negative consequences. Using computers requires knowledge and this knowledge is 'middle-class' knowledge. The introduction of CMC into the normal work of NGOs in the South may then strengthen middle-class NGOs and people with middle-class or academic backgrounds in those grassroots organizations that might adopt the technology. In either case, the losers would be those activists without the background and/or training necessary to utilize the new technology. While I do not agree with the conclusion that NGOs should avoid the new technology, the point is serious. Without much research to rely on here, one must fall back on immediate observation and experience. Based on my academic, computer-networking and NGO work in India, several experiences would point in a different direction.

The first observation is that the danger of the gentrification of NGOs is not specific to the introduction of CMC technology. It is probably endemic to the introduction of any new technology. My experiences with NGOs in India goes back to the mid-1960s. Then it was introducing typewriters and cyclostyles; the rare telephone (still) usually has a keylock on it. There is much mystification of the computer. So when I arrived with one out in a village centre, the big tease was that it could read everyone's thoughts and keep them all inside itself! This was, by the way, not my idea, but a popular fairy tale. But the slow process of learning to use the machine by the office women was also an empowerment – and the computer is a symbol of power. This gets complicated with organizational hierarchy, traditional values and male chauvinism. As elsewhere, men tend to run NGO organizations and women tend to do the secretarial work. So controlling the computer, a symbol of power, becomes important. But Indian bosses don't type – that's secretarial work. So a paradox arises out of the conflict of power, hierarchy and gender. The point being made is that every time an Indian woman uses a keyboard, she is performing an act of gender empowerment.

There is another aspect to this as well. One of the big problems facing south Indian Social Action Groups (SAGs) is the inability to recruit new leadership and support from within the middle class. In the 1960s and 1970s, radicals and progressives from the middle class forged alliances with the poor, giving rise to what is now a relatively successful movement for social change. The new Indian middle class, large, growing and consumer-bent, is producing a large number of computer literates and experts. I have noticed that some of these are drawn into social work because of the possibility of working with modern communications technology.

On a much more concrete level, there is a phenomenon that netweaver Mika Böök has dubbed 'ASCII imperialism': computer systems, especially small computer systems, developed in the English-speaking world. In the early days of computers, memory was at a premium and programmers were limited in the number of symbols that could be allowed. A standard was set up and adopted, ASCII (American Standard Code for Information Interchange). This was based on the English alphabet. Computer-mediated communications systems, transfer protocols and programs were set up to work on and with this basic ASCII (7-bit) code. Non-English letters and symbols had to be converted back and forth to comply with the ASCII standard. Technical developments have made it possible and feasible to go beyond this, allowing for other alphabets to find their place in the world of computer-mediated communications. But the old standard lingers on, much as we still type on our 'QWERTY' typewriters and keyboards – the layout of which was determined over a hundred years ago, when the first mechanical typewriters appeared. Since the key arms tended to tangle into each other, letters that were found together least frequently (in English) were put next to each other on the keyboard. This makes bad sense for typing speed, of course. And, likewise, ASCII imperialism played havoc on many a CMC system for a long time.

Another hurdle, embedded in the geographic metaphor, is the mapping mystique. Even NGOs fall back into the 'market share' frame of mind, forgetting that one of the main purposes and characteristics of CMC is that it collapses geography. Yet another hurdle facing computer-mediated systems is their very success. Networkers are under constant pressure from new groups to help them get 'online', and many systems have growth problems, especially from the fact that expenditures for expansion come before income from expansion. Another success problem is that many larger organizations or existing networks of common interest want their own computer-mediation communication system. Related to this may be a 'fishes and sharks' problem: for whatever reasons, actors appear who want either to gobble up successful areas of endeavour or, if unable to do this, at least to scatter the shoal.[15]

The progressive networkers and netweavers of computer-mediated communication have to steer between the pitfalls of commodification and statism. The use of modern information technology makes information more saleable. Since NGOs can increase their effectiveness by using ICT, it is not surprising that this technology has been spreading rapidly in this sector. And since technology is never value free, it is also not surprising that homesteaders appear, staking out rival 'better' claims. This is another illustration that the struggle over the mode of information is ever present. This struggle is being defined in terms of 'governance' of the new technology.[16]

It is in the nature of states to control and regulate. What is not so obvious is that interstate bodies also have this statist impetus – not just the bodies set up simply to regulate, but even the more benign international bodies, such as those in and around the United Nations. This control is exercised through the granting of 'status', a recognition of groups and organizations that often have been out in the political wasteland for a long time, and co-optation into various worthwhile projects. In other words, NGOs can be controlled by someone else defining the *agenda* for meaningful action. This of course applies to the NGOs' networkers, whose task is to service the information and communications needs of the broader NGO community. Agenda disruption can occur through net entropy:

creation of support to numerous 'nets' that may be no more than a website.

A website is not a network Just as a flashy folder does not make an organization, a website does not make a network. This is sometimes forgotten, since websites tend to look alike and it is possible for a single webmaster to give the impression that there is a big organization or even a network behind him.

Technological relapse into the broadcasting paradigm The 'new' computer-based technology is merging with the 'old' technologies of telephones, radio and television, in terms of both carriers and the equipment on the user end. Internet surfing can now be done on the television screen, with an accompanying possibility for simplistic email replies. One major purpose of this, of course, is for tele-marketing. This also opens the door for the 'alternative broadcasting' on a mass scale, just as cable and satellite television opened the door for the break-up of older monopolies. Yet new monopolies arose here and it is hardly surprising to find the big actors in the older media moving in to this new realm of WWW broadcasting.

One example of alternative broadcasting put into practice via the Internet is the One World 'WWW supersite'. Using European Union money, this site, operated by a group of ex-BBC media workers, is offering NGOs a channel where they can broadcast their materials, perhaps even expanding beyond the printed media into WWW-distributed audio and video clips. The 'supersite' databases materials from the organizations that they publish here as well as providing materials on topics concerning human rights and development issues. Part of their stated programme is to address the lopsided flow of information in the world, searching for ways to increase the South–South flow of information.[17]

This example brings out some of the contradictions in applying ICT to create one, better, world: there is a tendency to lapse into what Theodore Roszak calls 'the cult of information'. By this is meant the belief that information changes something. Paraphrasing Neil Postman, one could say that there is a danger of informing ourselves to death – that is, into inactivity. Another contradiction is that flashy presentation and delivery systems would strengthen the broadcasting paradigm, reducing the communication aspects of the technology. There is a definite danger of this as audio and video uses of ICT become more widespread for those who have access to the bandwidth. 'Web activism' becomes defined in terms of being properly informed, without the communicative element necessary for action.[18] By setting the technological entry level rather high in terms of equipment, connectivity and computer competence, such types of support to the South would only include a very small part of the Southern elites. As presented above, there are way of getting around this, but it would not appear to be from within the broadcasting paradigm.

As CMC moves out of its text-based forms and environments toward audio and video, both in real time (streaming) and as 'clips' that can be stored, new challenges are put on the doorstep of those who would put the possibilities in the service of social change. This means developing software (and sometimes hardware). One organization doing this is RealNetworks, formerly Progressive Networks, in Seattle, Oregon, in the USA. Their software package RealPlayer for audio and video is competing well with its Microsoft and Apple counterparts.[19] Through their WebActive project, they are plugging into progressive circles, albeit with a North American bias. Whether the Northern bias can be overcome and the communications dimension incorporated remains to be seen but there are tools being provided which could encourage developments in this direction.

Reactions from government

The anarchistic culture of hackerism frightened many people, including people in government. Criminal uses of the new computer technology have received wide publicity and many politicians have responded to the fear generated by proposing different kinds of policing, legislation and control systems. This seemed to be following the logic of judging a new technology on its misuse and perceived dangers rather than on its normal use or even possible better uses. Critics point out that much of the legislation, either intentionally or in effect, would curb not criminality but legitimate freedoms of speech and assembly. A first wave of reaction swept over the 'crackers' (criminal hackers) who spent their time breaking into closed computer systems and, in the case of some, even doing espionage or worse when they got there.[20] The next wave was directed against the pornographers (and worse) who had started using the Internet to push their pictures and prose on an under-age public. The US Congress passed legislation (which did not hold up in court) trying to curtail this use of the new medium. Reactions to this were two-fold: a digital free-speech movement was launched that proved itself to be a rather good lobbyist, with institutions such as the Electronic Frontier Foundation in the forefront. This Blue Ribbon Campaign is being jointly sponsored by the American Civil Liberties Union, the Electronic Frontier Foundation, and the Electronic Privacy Information Center. Another reaction was the development of software packages that would let parents and not some government do the Net-nannying of their children.

The US government, no doubt pressed by its police and security agencies, started proposing various ways of controlling and monitoring the new media. One such proposal described above was for a 'clipper chip' to be installed in electronic communications equipment that would allow an advanced wire-trapping by police authorities. This was eventually abandoned in its original form, but still there was a felt need for governments to find a way to monitor electronic communications as part of crime detection and prevention. Toward the end of 1997, the US government threw in the towel and announced that censorship will not be used; the Internet needs to be free, since this is good for business. However, there would still be a problem with encryption keys.[21]

Some governments were still going for censorship, though. Even Sweden, traditionally proud of its free speech and free assembly legislation, was trying to shackle CMC by introducing legislation making the carriers of electronic communication responsible for the content. The idea here was to equate BBSes with publications, making the 'editor' legally responsible for the material. The reaction was the same as to other such attempts to force self-censorship onto computer-mediated communication whose ethic maintains that it is the individual who is responsible for his or her words and deeds.[22] Yet Swedish legislation has been so out of date that uncensored minutes of city councils were not even allowed electronic publication.

Reactions from business

Ever since ICT started there has been a watershed between those who have seen the technology primarily in terms of broadcasting and those who have seen it in terms of communication. The new communications tools and channels opened up by developments such as PCs, low-cost modems, the Internet and the WWW were quickly grasped by many in the business community as a way of marketing and, for information products, distribution. Many websites finance themselves by providing advertising space. This process of transformation from communication to broadcasting is being accentuated in new 'push technologies' – pushing ads onto users, who are being transformed into Net-consumers. Established media giants such as CNN and FOX have been first out in pushing their broadcasts onto Net users, even in unordered 'packages' that accompany computer and communications packages.

The organization of meaning

> Information is not participation and communication is not democracy. Although access to both should be regarded as essential human rights, in themselves they lack any direction or option for sensibilisation without some form of context or analysis.
>
> Michael Polman, Antenna

A major drawback of computer-mediated communication is information overload, which leads quickly to information entropy and loss of meaning. How are the civil networks dealing with information overload? One way of managing information overload is host subdivision. Separate hosts are set up to collect, administer and distribute a pre-defined spectrum of information, often tied to a specific constituency. This became economically and technologically feasible with falling hardware costs and software that requires less technical expertise. Another dynamic is at work as well. Larger, 'established' organizations have started using ICT to improve and expand existing information channels and usage, especially with the arrival of the WWW and the spread of Internet connectivity into households in the North. Proliferation of hosts may be counterproductive to networking effectiveness, however, since navigating through a myriad of websites, even in a narrow interest area, may be difficult, especially if the area is politicized and selectively linked. So meta-linking through sites such as One World and the Institute for Global Communications becomes important for the retention of social meaning.

Other experiments are being made along the lines of easy-to-use and distributed database managers. The 'search engines' helping to de-confuse the WWW are relatively well known. Another experiment is with 'knowbots' an acronym for *knowledge robot*. The idea here is that since there is so much information available, organized along different principles and stored all over the globe, it is a waste of resources to do online searches or to distribute information databases. Instead the question, or query, is sent over the matrix. The knowbot is to be like a detective, roaming around in 'cyberspace' searching for clues, modifying the query and reporting back with some answers. This idea is an epistemological step forward. Instead of thinking like 'electronic librarians' in the Sisyphean task of cataloguing and piece-meal search, the problem is turned around. The task of the 'cyber-narian' (helmsman of knowledge) is to look for meaningful questions – the answers are out there waiting.

The long march through cyberspace

This study sheds some light on the question of whether the intro-duction of the new information technology is an independent, deter-mining factor in the appearance of a post-industrial 'information society', or the result of the needs of this emerging society. The emancipatory usage of computer-mediated communication points to the conclusion that the technology, applied under certain circum-stances and conditions, is such an independent factor. In its emanci-patory usage, information technology does not just reinforce already existing information flows; it creates new patterns, both of informa-tion and communication, and of consciousness and coalitions for change. Thus the hypothesis, proposed for example by David Dickson in his small classic *Alternative Technology and the Politics of Technical Change* (1974), that alternative technology presupposes an alternative society needs to be modified. It can now be proposed that alternative technology presupposes a *movement* toward an alter-native society. In other words, information technology can be an important cog in the wheels of change. This movement must be viewed dialectically, with a utopian momentum. A closing theoretical reflection on this will be presented.

The emerging 'information society' reflects and is a bearer of all the conflicts of the society from which it is emerging. Some would say that information technology enhances socio-economic differences and conflicts. Since these conflicts are real, they should be studied in such a way as to allow for the conflicts and contradictions to constitute empirical categories in a theoretical analysis. A theoretical approach that could be used here would come from the toolbox of utopian dialectics. 'Utopian' will be defined below. We will now take a closer look at what is meant by 'dialectic' before combining the two again.

'Dialectic' is an elastic term, shapable to many forms. It can be considered from many different perspectives and at many different levels of abstraction. This has been done by many for more than two millennia. Dialectic connotes dialogue, communication and interaction. Dialectics has to do with contradictions and opposites. These can be natural opposites, such as hot and cold. They can be social categories, such as gender. Contradictions can be real: for example, the fact that the richest country in the world produces an increasing number of poor and homeless. Contradictions can, of course, be very abstract.

Dialectics, as a method of analysis, deals with the nature of relationships between opposites and within sets of contradictions. Opposites are not merely negations of each other. Contradictions and conflicts manifest themselves at different levels and in different arenas of human experience. Conflict on one level or arena can reflect contradictions and conflicts in other levels or arenas. The reflection can be more or less homologous. It is in the deviation from total congruence that interesting and fruitful insights can arise concerning social and technological change. For example: Is 'cyberspace' being colonized in such a way as merely to replicate consumer/corporate capitalism or is there scope for other socio-economic patterns to arise? In what ways are movements for social change subjected to market and statist forces and imperatives?

What are the different levels of dialectical analysis? At the macro-level there is the polarity expressed in terms of hegemony and autonomy. This can be seen as the dominant, or primary, contradiction. The forces of hegemony, using *inter alia* the industrialization and monopolization of culture, try to form consciousness – the 'total ideology' of their societies, be they global, national or local. These 'forces' have names: Murdoch, Berlesconi, Time-Warner. Autonomy can be due to an unpenetrated state of affairs or as the result of a cultural and political struggle, which can carried on at the global, national or local level.

What is 'utopian'?

The term 'utopia' is usually credited to Sir Thomas More, who, in the early sixteenth century, described an imagined state, and state of affairs, in which men were what they were meant to be: civilized, kind and humane, fair and just. Actually, he was looking back toward disappearing norms. This professedly idealistic view of the possibilities of human nature was given rough treatment by materialists and determinists, who viewed the shape and causes of human behaviour in quite a different way. For many, and for many a year, 'utopian' became somewhat synonymous with 'unrealistic'. 'Utopian socialists' were seen to be esoteric escapists, whereas 'the real socialists' understood the workings of the real world and how to get a handle on these workings. Political history, social praxis and modern political analysis call for a revision of the definition of utopian.

The collapse of 'real' or state socialism and its democratic cousin, 'social engineering', demonstrated that the idea that men could really get a grasp on the steering wheel of history was, to say the least, unrealistic.[23] The socio-political praxis of many movements for social change in the twentieth century has showed, both in theory and in practice, that means generate ends. Examples here would be various anti-colonial movements for national independence and the civil rights movement in the United States.[24] A large and growing body of research in modern political science confirms the idea that means tend to create their own outcomes.[25] But this is moving too fast.

What is meant by the term 'utopia'? Its root meaning is 'some other place', being a combination of the Greek *ou* (not, nowhere) and *topos* (place). The concept of 'utopia' and 'utopian' can be understood thematically in two broad senses: the classical and the integrated. In his study *Utopisk dialektikk* (1976), Danish philosopher Ole Thyssen presents a fruitful discourse on the categories of utopia. The classical forms of utopia are interpreted as daydream, as idealization, as alternative and as preludium. Integrated utopia arises out of critical theory and praxis, the dialectical undercurrent of possibilities of the manifest. While classical utopia is other-worldly, or at least beyond present historical possibilities, integrated utopia is a function of history. Each of these forms of utopia will be given closer attention. This will be done as explication and as exemplification of information technological phenomena.

Utopia as daydream   The simplest form for utopia is flight, dreaming away from this world into a much better place. It is not the world that changes but me and my place in it.

> And this new place appears to me to be highly *possible* since I see it described every day: in advertisements, in the media, society's promises, briefly put, in all those adventures that a given society relates about it-self.[26]

The daydream does not try to change the world since it is concerned with a dream within the existent. In this sense it is highly subjective, and personal. This is unlike other forms for utopia that are collective. Since utopian daydreaming is based on loss or absence, it has a great potential for collective exploitation, a fact inherently understood by commercial interests. In the newspeak of info-tech this is called 'virtual reality'. In this multi-medial make-believe world, reality and the flight from it become totally personal, and isolated. Virtual reality is reflexive, commenting on itself, the seduced being fully conscious of what is happening. This is info-tech as amusement park.

Some telematic utopians have presented various aspects of information technology as a 'technological fix' for problems of late industrial society. In this brave new world of cyberspace everyone will be able to communicate with one another through electronic mail. Most people on this planet still do not have electricity much less telephones or computers. So this 'everyone' is highly qualified, meaning everyone who matters – that is, who has money and skill enough to join the ICT club. But this problem is 'solved' in the next form of utopia.

Utopia as idealization   Like the utopian daydream, utopian idealization remains tied to existing society. But it is a society purified of distasteful and unwanted traits. This cleansing is accomplished by separating society's 'true nature' from unwanted consequences of that society. For example, the exploitation of nature is seen as an abrogation of modernity and not as a *sine qua non* for the development of industrial society. A main characteristic of utopia as idealization is that results and intentions are disconnected: since the intent is good, any bad results that occur along the way, being unintentional, are not 'really' a part of the system, but blemishes easily corrected. If this cannot be done, then the faults lie with human nature and not with the system at hand. In this sense, idealization becomes 'ideology' – a systematic and theoretical legitimization for a given, or proposed, society.

In the world of info-tech, we can all become an ideal, with a cellular phone in hand, talking and/or plugged in to our laptop, communicating with others around the globe. If we cannot personally do this, due to unintended and irrelevant blemishes, then at least we can be comforted by the knowledge that we are part of a society in which this is happening.

Utopia as alternative   It is in the sense of alternative that the term 'utopia' is most widely understood. This is in contrast to idealization, which is the systematically purified form by which a society understands itself.[27] But even in the sense of alternative, or counter-society, there are many variations on the theme of utopia: the moral–religious utopias of Biblical prophets, Plato's ideal state, the utopias of various Greek philosophers, More, Bacon, Campanella, and so on.

There have been those utopians who have sought direct realization: for example anarchists who saw that the destruction of corrupt institutions (the state) would usher in utopia, and the constructionists who established alternative societies through the cultivation of a concept of social order. This cultivation could be through either the maximization of freedom or the maximization of social control. All these variations of utopia as alternative have one thing in common: they need a blueprint, a social architecture of how things – that is, social relationships – are to be arranged. And here lies their vulnerability. Blueprints tend to become static, losing contact with the dialectical process of change and development, a lack of empirical grounding that blocks implementation.

Utopia as preludium   'The future is here.' This is not only an ad gimmick to help sell the paraphernalia of info-tech but also a well-grounded theoretical statement of considerable status. The criticism presented by Marx, Engels and Lenin of the utopian socialists was that they did not know the way out of the present (capitalist) system nor the way to their utopia. The critics claimed to have found the way, in the scientific laws of historical and dialectical materialism. The analysis presented by Marx, Engels and Lenin, if not a complete road map to the promised land, were at least serious proposals for a way out of the capitalist desert.

The core idea here is summarized in Marx's epithelial statement that the present is pregnant with the future – that tendencies latent now will become manifest later. Taken as it is, this is just common sense. Marx, and others of course, put this idea to considerable theoretical work. Among the well-known weaknesses is that the way *to* the promised land (utopia, classless society or whatever) is not known and, as Popper argues, cannot be known since all (historical) knowledge is *post facto*. And Popper put a lasting stamp of utopian dreaming on *Realsocialismus*.

Integrated utopia as emancipatory experience   This critical examination of the concept of 'utopia' may seem to lead to a theoretical dead end. In one sense it does: while 'utopia' is and has been an important element in theoretical and ideological systems, attempts to define theoretically any utopia eventually break down. This is because 'utopia', being 'somewhere else', cannot be defined in theoretical terms that are bound to the here and now. Another way of stating this is to say that utopia, in the qualified sense, cannot be understood theoretically since there are no 'facts' to relate such a theory to. Attempts to construct utopias based on non-utopian theory (and thinking) have broken down. Thus classical utopia has lost its historical importance. Ole Thyssen provides a possible way of re-thinking utopia:

> Utopia is thus neither everything nor nothing. It is not the motor of history, even though it is part of the history making process as a primary and half-blind movement. As producer of guiding motives [Leitmotiv] and as identifier of the unstated, it is a necessary and problematic com- ponent of every projection of the future and in every attempt to avoid that the future be merely a repetition of the past. To give up utopia is the same as binding oneself to the past.[28]

There may be another way to understanding utopia, using a dialectical approach. Utopia is a statement that the world can be different from what it is. Some might say that it is a systematization of hope. It is a construction. The root of utopia in its qualified definition is that of dialectic negation of the existent out of which contrary tendencies become manifest.

> The second phase, or movement of 'utopia' is thus no longer to describe a society separate from and in opposition to the present one, but on the

contrary to describe and criticize present society and *by this* act in a uto-pian manner – through the construction of the criteria and concepts that provide theoretical access to this society and through the deletion of the movement of society; and it is in this identification of the direction of movement that the description necessarily becomes 'utopian' in the new sense of the term.[29]

This study has been done within 'the context of discovery': ex-ploring movements that may represent the integrated type of utopia described above. Posing questions of a normative character, survey-ing experience and the generation of categories and new questions has been the primary goal. A hypothesis has been generated – that CMC networking strengthens the periphery. The testing of the hy-potheses moves us into the 'context of justification' and beyond the resources of the present endeavour.

It should be apparent to the reader that the possibilities of in-formation technology as applied networking for socio-political change has been viewed from an 'activist' perspective. The danger here is that working to make something happen may tend to make one see it happen. Hopefully, this pitfall has been tempered by analytical self-criticism. What is lacking in this regard from this author will surely be complemented by others in the ongoing, and online, discourse on the meaning and direction of the 'better' uses of information technology.

An important thesis of this study is that *autonomy* is an important component of the hacker ethic, a component that became embedded in the technology and the culture surrounding the technology. This is true for the movement of communications activists. It is also multi-dimensional. One important aspect is maintaining technological independence. Since 'the road ahead' for the lords of the global village is staked out in signposts of monopoly, or cyberocracy, main-taining a free technology is crucial.

Showdown at the Java corral

Since the World Wide Web is expected to become a major area for market expansion, it is here that conflicts could be expected to surface. In 1994, the US Department of Justice and Microsoft reached an out-of-court agreement whereby Microsoft promised not to mis-use its monopoly position in terms of operating systems. When Microsoft decided to include its Internet Explorer as an integral part of its operating system (OS) package, the Department of Justice reacted and took Microsoft to court. The question raised was whether or not this was a monopolistic attempt to force consumers into the Microsoft fold, putting the main competitor Netscape into a position of disadvantage. In December 1997, a court decision – immediately appealed – went against Microsoft. But this may just be a minor detour on the road ahead to global monopoly for Microsoft. The case chosen, although symbolically important, was just the tip of the iceberg. Microsoft already had over 90 per cent of the market for operating systems for PCs, so one might have expected a legal challenge on the basis of anti-trust legislation to question this point, not the use or misuse of the monopoly. This was the obvious framework for action against Microsoft, especially given the Apple–Microsoft deal in mid-1997 and Microsoft's buying into various activities in the IT sector.[30]

The case of a packaged or non-packaged WWW browser became the focus of anti-trust activities by the US government, probably precipitated by an experienced breach of an agreement and monopolistic positioning. The anti-trust trial against Microsoft seemed to be turning into The Trial, at least for business, at the end of the decade. Whether or not the US government will break up Microsoft into a number of 'Baby Bills', parallel to what happened in telecom, is an open question. It may also be beside the question, since the dispute goes deeper than 'just' the question of company share in a particular market. It goes right to the heart of what form information society will be taking: open or controlled. In this sense, challenges to Microsoft's monopolistic tendencies were coming from other areas.[31]

The development of the Java programming language and its application to the WWW seemed to be the fulfilment of a guiding philosophy of SUN Microsystems (Stanford University Networks): that the network is the computer. With Java, distributed computing on a global basis, irrespective of system platform, was becoming a foreseeable possibility. In order for this to work, a standard Java was needed so that the whole of the Net would truly become like one computer. Put in another way, the future operating system could become 'netwide'; so controlling the tools for developing this netwide operating system is strategically crucial. So SUN took out its own brand of 'copyleft' copyright that said that second parties could package Java but not charge for it and above all not change it.[32]

Bill Gates and Scott McNealy have been taking a page from Marx and Engels: the battle for Java's future has turned to class warfare. Things got ugly at last week's Java Internet Business Expo, meant to showcase Java's growing maturity for practical applications, as Microsoft officials ripped into Sun's newly issued Java classes and made moves to splinter Java development.

Microsoft is offering its Application Foundation Classes (AFC) – a set of ready-to-use building blocks for Java applications – as an alternative to the Java Foundation Classes (JFC) Sun provides in its latest revision of the Java Developer's Kit (JDK). More than that, it plans to include the AFC in new versions of Internet Explorer – and says it won't ship or support the latest version of the JDK.[33]

Microsoft announced plans to include its own AFC with the Internet Explorer application it was trying to get accepted as an integral part of its OS/Windows package. If Microsoft could force dealers to take its browser it would also be distributing its own brand of tools for a Net, or Web OS. This point is of strategic, paramount importance since the 'next phase' of the computer revolution being heralded is that of the IC, the Internet Computer. Some may see this as a step back to a netwide mainframe situation, with loss of control embedded in the personal computer. Others see it as the wave of the future, with distributed processing offering all users access to everything available.

In late 1997 SUN took Microsoft to court on the issue, the concrete legal point being to stop Microsoft from putting its variation under the Java logo.[34] Expectations were for a long litigation since the core issue was whether or not the tools determining the development of a Net OS would be free or not – free in the sense of free speech and not owned. In November 1998, SUN was granted a court injunction against Microsoft on the Java issue.[35] This parallels the challenge to monopoly coming from the Linux community.

It will be recalled that Linux is a free operating system with a solid base among computer programmers and developers. Proceeding from the assumption that computer technologists are a key group in the development of computer technology, computer consultant and writer Doc Searls argues the following:

Today, Linux is the technologists' OS. It's bad idea to bet against them. It's a good idea to bet with them. That's exactly what Netscape did when they released their source code to what everyone suddenly calls the Open

Source community, but for years was the Free Software movement. Significantly, Linux is free. But more significantly, Linux's source code is open. Anybody can look at it, tweak it and share their tweaks with friends – which is exactly why Linux is so popular with techies. Quite literally, it's theirs. They made it. ...

Lest we forget, the Internet was created by technologists, and its explosive growth is far more an expression of rampant hackery than of commercial activity, personal expression, massive archiving or whatever.

Consider this: over half of all the web pages on the Internet today are produced by free web software – mostly Apache – running on Linux operating systems.[36]

While the share of hosts running Linux may be exaggerated, these statements from the world of computing are quite important for our understanding of emerging patterns of politics of information and communication technology. What we are witnessing is the development of a distributed knowledge system in the mode of information that is socially, or 'collectively', owned. This 'ownership' is not based on jurisprudence or state protection but on community, the rights of the commons. It is perhaps too early to say where this will lead. But it is safe to say that it will have political repercussions since the field of activity here is the heart (or brain) of information society.

Microsoft has taken up the challenge posed by Linux – sometimes in ways that have sent shudders through the computing community and even parts of the mainstream press. When some of Microsoft's internal materials were leaked in 1998, under the name of the 'Halloween Documents', many started wondering what was in this bag of tricks. For the documents, confirmed by Microsoft as authentic but not necessarily company policy, revealed a way of thinking about competitors and alternative modes of thought concerning information and communication technology that seemed to be sorely out of step with the ethos of computing, the 'mindshare' of developers that the actors are out for. And, as Eric S. Raymond, who burst open the documents for public scrutiny, points out, attempts to 'de-commoditize protocols' are a keypin for maintaining a system of monopolistic profit. What this means in non-computerese is that a situation in which operating systems, 'languages' for programming and communication and the like, are separate packages subjected to open review, modification and competition favours both the consumer and the development of the industry.[37]

Whatever the immediate outcomes, or non-outcomes, of the litigation over monopolies, copyrights and censorship taking place at the end of the century, a pattern is emerging – or rather re-emerging, for it is the old question of freedom of expression and assembly. In the socio-technological space of the Internet and the World Wide Web now, there are the libertarians who maintain that the tools of expression must remain free, those who fear misuse, and those who want a controlled market. It is in this pattern of interests and conflicts that we have to start looking for an emerging new polity of information society.

Cyberwars

There have been predictions of coming 'cyberwars'. What this might mean exactly differs from augurer to augurer, meaning one thing to RAND Corporations analysts, another thing to scholars concerned either about the governability of cyberspace or an encroaching cyberocracy, and still another thing to frightened journalists worried about their credit card numbers. Yet one thing these seem to have in common is the growing awareness that 'cyberspace' – what I have called the mode of information in ICT – is a field of conflict. It is more than a question of 'winning hearts and minds', in the sense of acceptance, adherence or rejection. It is a matter of conscientization in a deeper sense, the empowering realization that the oneness of the globe is not just an abstract idea or goal but an everyday reality.

The cyber-methodology of the 'keyboard warriors' is the nonviolent, electronic struggle over the mode of information. The methodology of the communication activists studied here has several basic components, working within a given framework. The game strategy for scoring on this field of conflict consists of the availability of email, for protected inter-personal communication; of communication tools such as conferencing and mailinglists for inter-organizational exchange of information, discourse and coordination of activities; of tools such as websites for distribution of materials to a broader public and databasing tools for the construction of a knowledge base and community memory. The framing factors are two: the technology must be freely available and the sociology must work. The hackers, old and new, have provided a free technological base upon which to work – and one that is developing parallel to its emancipatory applications. The sociology is one of commitment to making the world a better place. In my decades of work and research with communications activists I have found no evidence of a belief in a technological fix. Rather I have found the understanding that it is in the synergetic meeting of social movements with a new technology that empowerment occurs. ICT adds an element of self-awareness of belonging to a network of people working for the same or similar cause. 'Communities of purpose' or 'intentional communities' develop quickly and on a global scale. The farmer in India, while not presently engaged in the cyber struggle, is surely affected by its outcome. For example, by multinationals databasing his traditional farming and herbal knowledge to secure intellectual property rights on what he considers common knowledge. As he is being exposed to the world market, he too will be joining his fishermen colleagues, organizing for example in, yes, 'FishNet' (Trivandrum), part of a global online network of small fishermen.

So what?

This study has shown that there is an electronic fabric of struggle for humanization. Issues can be put on the global agenda and campaigns become 'successful' in an informational sense, using the new WWW and Internet technologies. At least five-plus-one components seem to be necessary for a concern to become a sustained 'issue' on the global informational and awareness agenda:

1. *email* penetration;
2. electronic *newsletter*(s) for distribution of crucial information to activists;
3. an electronic *forum* for information sharing and discussion and strategic planning among activists;
4. an *archive* for easy retrieval of data in the issue area;
5. a *WWW site* providing a publishing showcase and easy point of entry for both casual and more serious information-seekers, as well as linkages to related sites and material.

The 'plus-one' component is the existence of informational and organizational links for spreading material and coordinating activities in offline mode. In other words, the 'better' uses of ICT do not happen in a vacuum but in social and political contexts as part of the process of change.

Access to the new ICT is heavily concentrated in the North, and even here among the more affluent and influential, and in the South, among an even narrower elite. What this means for one thing is that the elites in the world are increasingly interconnected and inter-informed. It means, for example, that the arrest of a leader of the democratic opposition in Burma becomes something of a household concern among a considerable portion of the elite. By definition it is this elite that governs the world. The struggle over, and in, the new mode of information is showing that this governance is becoming more and more transparent. When democratic countries try to bolster up the economy of undemocratic Burma, there is protest and economic unrest. In one sense, the elites are the most susceptible to 'cyber warfare' since this type of struggle is in their medium and shaped by this medium into a rationality that is familiar.

The conflict is not just ideological, between the good guys and the bad guys, usually defined in terms of oppression, exploitation and political, social and economic justice. There is something more. It is also a struggle about a deep-rooted fear of disorder. It is a fear not only between people but also within people. This fear, according to philosopher Stephen Toulmin, was a major driving force behind the social construction that we call 'modernity'. Playing upon this fear can be an effective way of co-opting liberal intellectuals into the task of maintaining 'order' – that is, hierarchy – in cyberspace.

The original hacker pioneers opened the way for making the computer revolution personal. They broke the technology out of closed culture and control of the military–industrial complex. The extension of this into the field of meaningful social action is found in the work of the communication activists. They have injected the element of social meaning into information and communication technology. By demonstrating that ICT can be used for non-commercial purposes, the communication activists have created an ethical point of reference in contrast to those who would make the shopping mall the norm for human activity.

At the beginning of this study a question was put regarding what beyond the obvious better uses of information and communication technology might be supported or induced. This is a matter of questioning – that is, of discovering what to look for and where. If there is any 'where' any more. For what the examples presented here have shown is the emergence of a new synergetic 'cognitive space' for social action: distributed knowledge systems that are both a-synchronic and glocal. Out of time and space. Experiences and ideas about what needs to be done are recorded, enabling both cumulative social action and action research. The global and the local merge into 'glocality', with CMC systems providing empowering tools for the realization of the old slogan of thinking globally and acting locally.

What this means analytically is a tendency toward universalism; in the terms of the progressive values of this study, a process of humanization in the broad sense. An example is the universalistic application of a set of basic human rights that is propelling much social action at the turn of the millennium. The serious questions that need to be put deal with issues of the imposition of a world culture on the local – something surely happening full force without computer-mediated communication. In the words of many communication activists: how can the new technology be used to give voice to culturally specific forms of knowledge?

Notes

1. Murray Edelman, *Politics as Symbolic Action*, Chicago 1971.
2. See Jürgen Habermas, *The Theory of Communicative Action*, Cambridge 1984.
3. One Italian-based system is called, simply, agora.
4. At <http://kows.web.net/udc/index.html>.
5. Graham Lane, *Communications for Progress*, Nottingham 1990.
6. The two top posts at the *Linux Journal* are held by women (mid-1998).
7. See Mika Böök, 'Fredsnätet och kriget vid Persiska viken' (PeaceNet and the Gulf War), in *Press i klipp, fil och forsk* (The Press in Clipping, File and Research), Helsinki 1991, pp. 143–52.
8. See Lars Ingelstam and Lennart Sturesson (eds), *Brus över landet: om informationsöverflödet, kunskapen och människan* (Noise over the land: About overabundant information, knowledge and the human condition), Stockholm 1993.
9. Stephen Toulmin, *Cosmopolis – The Hidden Agenda of Modernity*, New York 1990.
10. See Chris C. Demchák, 'Cyberspace and Emergent Body Politic', *Policy Currents*, vol. 4, no. 4, 1994, pp. 1, 6–9.
11. Michael Polman, 'Electronic Media, Revolutions and Totalitarianism – An Essay on NGOs and the Global Village', *InterDoc Europe Newsletter*, no. 5, pp. 4–7.
12. See *Scientific American*, September 1991.
13. Douglas R. Hofstadter, *Gödel, Escher, Bach: An Eternal Golden Braid*, London 1979.

14. Polman, 'Electronic Media, Revolutions and Totalitarianism'.

15. This problem, and terminology, was suggested to me by Michael Polman.

16. See, for example, Brian D. Loader (ed.), *The Governace of Cyberspace: Politics, Technology and Global Restructuring*, London 1997.

17. At <http://www.oneworld.org>.

18. An example of this is the 'WebActive' project of what was formerly called Progressive Networks, now Real Networks, Inc., that are producing a high-quality tool for audio and video over the Internet, Real Audio/ Video.

19. Realizing this, Microsoft has been buying into RealNetworks. See MS-Watch newsgroup.

20. Bruce Sterling, *The Hacker Crackdown*, New York 1992; Cliff Stoll, *The Cuckoo's Egg*, New York 1989.

21. *Dagens Nyheter*, 19 November 1997; announcement by White House spokesperson Ira Magaziner.

22. See critical discussion presented by local computer club in Tyresö, for example Ragnar Gyberg, 'Elektronisk yttrandefrihet', Institutionen för Datavetenskap Linköpings Universitet, 1996.

23. See Karl Popper, *The Open Society and Its Enemies*, vols 1 and 2, 5th edn, London 1966.

24. See Joan Bondurant, *The Conquest of Violence: The Gandhian Philosophy of Conflict*, Princeton 1958; Eric H. Ericson, *Gandhi's Truth: On the Origins of Militant Nonviolence*, New York 1969.

25. This is the field of implementation research. For some changes in the discipline, see Henrik P. Bang, 'Politics as Praxis. A New Trend in Political Science', *Statsvetenskaplig tidskrift* 1989, pp. 75–89.

26. Thyssen, *Utopisk dialektikk*, p. 128.

27. Ibid., p. 145.

28. Ibid., p. 168.

29. Ibid., p.170.

30. See *Time*, 18 August 1997; a special 'M$-Watch' group has appeared, which is monitoring Microsoft's road ahead. See also Microsoft Watch: <http://www.mercurycenter.com/business/microsoft/>.

31. Trial updates are at: <http://www.techweb.com/wire/features/1998/ microsoftTrial>.

32. See Ian G. Jacobs, 'Java Wars: Sun–Microsoft Feud Keeps on Brewing', *VAR Business*, no. 1315, 1 September 1997.

33. Owen Thomas, 'CLASS WARFARE Microsoft and SUN offer competing Java Libraries, to the Dismay of Developers', *Red Herring*, 2 September 1997.

34. The SUN position is found at their website: <http://www.sun.com/>.

35. At <http://www.sun.com/announcement/ruling.html>.

36. Doc Searls, 'Betting on Darwin', *Linux Journal*, August 1998, p. 12.

37. See Eric S. Raymond's comments to the 'Halloween Documents', published together at <www.opensource.org/halloween1.html>.

Select Sources

Abramson, Jeffrey B., et al., *The Electronic Commonwealth: The Impact of New Media Technologies on Democratic Politics*, New York 1988.

Annis, Sheldon, 'Giving Voice to the Poor', *Foreign Policy*, no. 84, Fall 1991, pp. 93–106.

Bagdikian, Ben H., 'The Lords of the Global Village', *The Nation*, 12 June 1989.

Bagdikian, Ben H., *The Media Monopoly*, New York 1992.

Bang, Henrik P., 'Politics as Praxis. A New Trend in Political Science', *Stats-vetenskaplig tidskrift*, 1989, pp. 75–89.

Bates, Benjamin J., 'The Role of Social Values in Information Policy: The Cases of France and Japan', *Information and Behavior*, no. 2, 1988, pp. 288–307.

Beamish, Anne, 'Communities On-Line: Community Based Computer Networks', MIT, February 1995. At: <http://alberti.mit.edu/arch/4.207/anneb/thesis/toc.html>.

Becker, Jörg (ed.), *Information Technology and a New International Order*, Lund 1984.

Bettelheim, Bruno, *The Uses of Enchantment: The Meaning and Importance of Fairy Tales*, New York 1977.

Bonchek, Mark S., 'Grassroots in Cyberspace: Using Computer Networks to Facilitate Political Participation', The Political Participation Project, MIT Artificial Intelligence Laboratory, Presented at the 53rd Annual Meeting of the Midwest Political Science Association, Chicago IL, on 6 April 1995 (also online).

Brants, Kees, 'The Social Construction of the Information Revolution', *European Journal of Communication*, vol. 4, no. 1, March 1989, pp. 79–97.

Böök, Mika, *Nätbyggaren: En undersökning av den moderna posten* (The Net-builder: A Survey of Modern Mail), Helsinki 1989.

Böök, Mika, 'Fredsnätet och kriget vid Persiska viken' (PeaceNet and the Gulf War'), in *Press i klipp, fil och forsk* (The Press in Clipping, File and Research), Helsinki 1991, pp. 143–52.

Böök, Mika, 'SOVIET COUP On-line at the Front-line', *InterDoc Europe Newsletter*, no. 5, October 1991.

Carey, Alex, *Taking The Risk Out of Democracy: Corporate Propaganda versus Freedom and Liberty*, reprint, University of Illinois 1997.

Castells, Manuel, *The Information Age: Economy, Society and Culture*, 3 vols., Oxford 1997.

Chakravarty, Pradip and Sunita Vasudeva, 'Communications Research: One Paradigm or Plurality of Views? Taking Stock of a Discipline', *Social Action*, vol. 41, no. 2, April–June 1991, pp. 176–95.

de Sola Pool, Ithial, *Technologies of Freedom*, Cambridge 1983.

Demchák, Chris C., 'Cyberspace and Emergent Body Politic', *Policy Currents*, vol. 4, no. 4, 1994.

Dewey, John, *Democracy and Education*, New York 1916.

Dickson, David, *Alternative Technology and the Politics of Technical Change*, Glasgow 1974.

Duch, Raymond M., 'The Politics of Investment by the Nationalized Sector', *Western Political Quarterly*, vol. 43, no. 2, June 1990, pp. 245–65.

Edelman, Murray, *Politics as Symbolic Action*, Chicago 1971.

Eneroth, Bo, *Hur mäter man vackert?* (How Do You Measure Beautiful?), Gothenburg 1989.

Etzioni, Amitai, *The Spirit of Community*, New York 1993.

Felsenstein, Lee, 'The Commons of Information', *Dr Dobb's Journal*, May 1993, pp. 18–24.

Fernandez, Leo and Somen Chakraborty, 'Social Impact of Information–Communication Technologies', *Social Action*, vol. 48, no. 3, July–September 1998, pp. 253–67.

Frederick, Howard H., 'Computer Communications in Cross-Border Coalition-Building: North American NGO Networking Against NAFTA', *Gazetta*, 1992, no. 50, pp. 217–41.

Frederick, Howard H., 'Computer Networks and the Emergence of Global Civil Society: The Case of the Association for Progressive Communications (APC)', in Linda Harasim and Jan Walls (eds), *Globalizing Networks: Computers and International Communication*, Cambridge 1993.

Frederick, Howard H., *Global Communication and International Relations*, Belmont CA 1997.

Galtung, Johan, 'A Structural Theory of Imperialism' in I. Vogeler and A.R. DeSouza (eds), *Dialectics of Third World Development*, New York 1980.

Habermas, Jürgen, *The Theory of Communicative Action*, Cambridge 1984.

Hamelink, Cees, *World Communication – Disempowerment and Self-Empowerment*, London 1995.

Harcourt, Wendy (ed.), *Women@internet*, London 1999.

Henderson, Hazel, 'Global Networks', *IN CONTEXT*, no. 36, Fall 1993; also online at <http://www.context.org/ICLIB/IC36/Hendersn.htm>.

Herman, Edward S. and Noam Chomsky, *Manufacturing Consent: The Political Economy of the Mass Media*, New York 1988.

Hiltz, Starr Roxanne, and Murray Turof, 'Structuring Computer-Mediated Communication Systems to Avoid Information Overload', *Communications of the ACM*, vol. 28, no. 7, July 1985, pp. 680–89.

Holub, Renate, *Antonio Gramsci: Beyond Marxism and Postmodernism*, London 1992.

Hofstadter, Douglas R., *Gödel, Escher, Bach: An Eternal Golden Braid*, London 1979.

178 In the Net

Iacono, Suzanne and Rob Kling, 'Computerization Movements and Tales of Technological Utopianism', in Rob Kling (ed.), *Computerization and Controversy: Value Conflicts and Social Choices*, 2nd edn, London 1995.

Ilshammar, Lars and Ola Larsmo, *net.wars*, Smedjebacken 1997.

Ingelstam, Lars and Lennart Sturesson (eds), *Brus över landet: om informationsöverflödet, kunskapen och människan* (Noise over the land: about overabundant information, knowledge and the human condition), Stockholm 1993.

Jones, Steven G. (ed.), *CyberSociety – Computer-Mediated Communication and Community*, London 1995.

Jones, Steven G. (ed.), *Virtual Culture – Identity and Communication in Cybersociety*, London 1997.

Lane, Graham, *Communications for Progress*, Nottingham 1990.

Leebart, Derak (ed.), *Technology 2001: The Future of Computing and Communications*, Cambridge 1991.

Li, Tiger, 'Computer-Mediated Communications and the Chinese Students in the U.S.', *Information Society*, vol. 7, 1990, pp. 125–37.

Loader, Brian D. (ed.), *The Governance of Cyberspace: Politics, Technology and Global Restructuring*, London 1997.

Longuet, Gérard, 'The World Battle of Telecommunications', *Politique internationale*, no. 34, Winter 1986–87, pp. 193–202.

MacBride, Sean, *One World, Many Voices*, Paris 1980.

MacLuhan, Marshall, *Understanding Media: The Extension of Man*, New York 1964.

MacLuhan, Marshall, and Bruce R. Powers, *The Global Village: Transformations in World Life and Media in the 21st Century*, Oxford 1989.

Madsen, Bent and Arne Mortensen, *Computermagt og menneskevaerd* (Computer Power and Human Value), Copenhagen 1985.

Negroponte, Nicholas, *being digital*, New York 1995.

Mosco, Vincent and Janet Wasko (eds), *The Political Economy of Information*, Madison WI and London 1988.

Polman, Michael, 'Electronic Media, Revolutions and Totalitarianism – An Essay on NGOs and the Global Village', *Interdoc Europe Newsletter*, no. 5, September 1991, pp. 4–7.

Popper, Karl, *The Open Society and Its Enemies*, vols 1 and 2, 5th edn, London 1966.

Postman, Neil, *Technopoly – The Surrender of Culture to Technology*, New York 1993.

Preston, Shelley, 'The 1992 Rio Summit and Beyond', *Swords and Ploughshares*, vol. 3, no. 2, Spring 1994; also online.

Quarterman, John S., *The Matrix: Computer Networks and Conferencing Systems Worldwide*, Bedford MA 1990.

Qvortrup, Lars, *The Social Significance of Telematics*, Amsterdam and Philadelphia 1984.

Rogers, Everett, et al., *Communication Technology: The New Media in Society*, New York 1987.

Roszak, Theodore, *The Cult of Information*, New York 1986.

Sallin, Susanne, 'The Association for Progressive Communications: A Cooperative Effort to Meet the Information Needs of Non-Governmental Organizations', Progressive Harvard–CIESIN Project of Global Environmental Change Information Policy, 14 February 1994.

Salvaggio, Jerry L. (ed.), *The Information Society – Economical, Social and Structural Issues*, New York 1989.

Samarajiwa, Rohan, 'The New Information Order: Retrospect and Prospect', *Tiers Monde* III, July–September 1987, pp. 677–86.

Scientific American, Special issue on Communications, Computers and Networks, September 1991.

Searls, Doc, 'Betting on Darwin', *Linux Journal*, August 1998.

Shamsuddin, M., 'The New World Information Order', *Pakistan Horizon*, vol. 40, no. 1, 1987, pp. 80–94.

Shamsuddin, M., 'UNESCO and the Flow of Information: A Case Study', *Pakistan Horizon*, vol. 40, no. 2, April 1988, pp. 31–49.

Sharples, Mike and Thea van der Geest (eds), *The New Writing Environment: Writers at Work in a World of Technology*, London 1996.

Slack, Jennifer Daryl and Fred Fejer (eds), *The Ideology of the Information Age*, Norwood NJ 1987.

Slouka, Mark, *War of the Worlds – Cyberspace and the High-tech Assault on Reality*, New York 1995.

Starkey, Paul, *networking for development*, London 1997.

Stenfield, Charles W., 'Computer-mediated Communications Systems', *Annual Review of Information Science and Technology*, 1986, pp. 21–68.

Sterling, Bruce, *The Hacker Crackdown*, New York 1992.

Stoll, Cliff, *The Cuckoo's Egg*, New York 1989.

Soumenin, Henrik and Tomas Walch, *Saga mot verklighet* (Fairy Tales of Reality), Stockholm 1998.

Thyssen, Ole, *Utopisk dialektik*, Copenhagen 1976.

Thyssen Ole and Mihail Larsen, *Menneske ret* (The Rights of Man), Haslev 1983.

Thyssen, Ole, *Nutiden: Det overfyldte rum* (The Present: The Overcrowded Room), Haslev 1993.

Toulmin, Stephen, *Cosmopolis – The Hidden Agenda of Modernity*, New York 1990.

Traber, Michael (ed.), *The Myth of the Information Revolution – Social and Ethical Implications of Communication Technology*, London 1986.

Vallée, Jacques, *The Network Revolution, Confessions of a Computer Scientist*, Berkeley 1982.

Webber, Douglas, et al., 'Information Technology and Economic Recovery in Western Europe: The Role of the British, French and West German Governments', *Policy Sciences*, vol. 19, no. 3, October 1986, pp. 319–46.

Westin, Alan F. (ed.), *Information Technology in a Democracy*, Cambridge 1971.

Woodhouse, Edward, 'New Section Project: The Political (Re)Construction of Technology', *Science and Technology Studies Newsletter* (American Political Science Association), vol. 5, no. 1, December 1992.

Zuboff, Shoshana, *In the Age of the Smart Machine: The Future of Work and Power*, New York 1988.

Webography

Computer Support for Social Action

Supersites

Institute for Global Communications   <http://www.igc.apc.org>
OneWorld Online   <http://www.oneworld.org/>
United Nations   <http://www.un.org>
Human Rights Watch   <http://www.hrw.org/>

In action, just a few examples...

Former Yugoslavia in Cyberspace   <http://www.igc.apc.org/balkans/web1.
html>
B92 Open Yugoslavia   <http://www.freeb92.net>
Third World Network/Southbound   < www.twnside.org.sg>

Women's nets

Women's Net at IGC   <http://www.igc.org/igc/womensnet/>
Southern Africa Women'sNet   <http://womensnet.org.za>
SAWNET (South Asian Women's NET)   <http://www.umiacs.umd.edu/users/
sawweb/sawnet/>
Global Fund for Women   <http://www.igc.apc.org/gfw/>
Russian Feminism Resources: <http://www.geocities.com/Athens/2533/
russfem.html>
The Independent Committee on Women and Global Knowledge (a consortium
of networks in Canada)   <http://www.postindustrial.com/morewomen/
index.html>

CMC Research and Discussion

John December's CMC resource site   <http://www.december.com>
'Occasio' Digital Social History Archive at the International Institute of Social
History   <http://www.iisg.nl/~occasio/>

Computer Lib and Co-ordination

Linux: The Linux Resources <http://www.linuxresources.com/>
Free Software Foundation <http://www.ptf.com/free/orgs/RO/P/FSF.html>
Open Source <http://www.opensource.org/>
Electronic Frontier Foundation <http://www.eff.org/>
Internet Society <http://www.isoc.org/>

The Other News and Webcasting

InterPress Service, IPS <http://www.ips.org/>
WebActive <http://www.webactive.com>
Freespeech Internet television network <www.freespeech.org>

Lest we Forget

Simon Wiesenthal Center <http://www.wiesenthal.com/index.html>
  (Contains the Center's own materials plus links to other Holocaust materials,
  including teachers' guides, as well as a 'Hate Watch' project to protect the
  Internet.)

Tools

Pegasus Mail <http://www.pegasus.usa.com/>
Netscape <home.netscape.com>
REAL software for audio/video <http://www.real.com>
Free Agent: (for following and organizing newsgroups/conferences) <http://
  www.forteinc.com>
Support and guides for working online <http://www.web.net/>

Compiled October–December 1998

Index

Page numbers in italics refer to illustrations